Diabetic Air Fryer Cookbook for Beginners UK

1600 Days Healthy & Budget Friendly Diabetic Recipes for Balanced Meals and Healthy Living without Sacrificing Taste | with 30-Day Meal Plan

Bruce M. Donald

Copyright© 2023 By Bruce M. Donald All Rights Reserved

This book is copyright protected. It is only for personal use. You cannot amend, distribute, sell, use, quote or paraphrase any part of the content within this book, without the consent of the author or publisher.

Under no circumstances will any blame or legal responsibility be held against the publisher, or author, for any damages, reparation, or monetary loss due to the information contained within this book, either directly or indirectly.

Disclaimer Notice:

Please note the information contained within this document is for educational and entertainment purposes only. All effort has been executed to present accurate, up to date, reliable, complete information. No warranties of any kind are declared or implied. Readers acknowledge that the author is not engaged in the rendering of legal, financial, medical or professional advice. The content within this book has been derived from various sources. Please consult a licensed professional before attempting any techniques outlined in this book.

By reading this document, the reader agrees that under no circumstances is the author responsible for any losses, direct or indirect, that are incurred as a result of the use of the information contained within this document, including, but not limited to, errors, omissions, or inaccuracies.

Contents

Introduction 1
Chapter One 2
Chapter 2 3
Chapter 3 4

Chapter 1   Breakfast 7
Air Fryer Breakfast Burrito 7
Air Fryer Cinnamon French Toast Sticks ... 7
Air Fryer Omelette 8
Air Fryer Breakfast Hash 8
Air Fryer Cinnamon French Toast 8
Air Fryer Egg and Veggie Muffins 9
Air Fryer Sweet Potato Toast 9
Air Fryer Blueberry Muffins 10
Air Fryer French Toast Sticks 10
Air Fryer Breakfast Sausage Patties 10
Air Fryer Cinnamon Apple Chips 11
Air Fryer Breakfast Stuffed Peppers 11
Air Fryer Banana Oatmeal Muffins 12
Air Fryer Turkey and Spinach Frittata 12
Air Fryer Blueberry Scones 13
Air Fryer Sweet Potato Hash Browns 13
Air Fryer Greek Omelette 14
Air Fryer Coconut Flour Pancakes 14
Air Fryer Apple Cinnamon Oatmeal 15
Air Fryer Baked Oats 15
Air Fryer Breakfast Quiche 16
Air Fryer Breakfast Burritos 16

Chapter 2 Main Recipes 17
Chicken Breasts 17
Air Fryer Fish Fillets 17
Turkey and Vegetable Skillet 17
Air Fryer Salmon 18
Air Fryer Turkey Burgers 18
Air Fryer Pork Chops 18
Air Fryer Beef Kabobs 19
Air Fryer Chicken Thighs 19
Air Fryer Chicken Parmesan 19
Salmon with Lemon-Dill Sauce 20
Air Fryer Beef and Broccoli Stir-Fry 20
Air Fryer Lemon Garlic Chicken 21
Air Fryer Fish Tacos with Mango Salsa 21
Air Fryer Lemon Herb Salmon with Roasted Vegetables 22
Air Fryer Tandoori Chicken Skewers: 22
Garlic Prawns and Broccoli 23
Air Fryer Chicken Fajitas 23
Airfryer Pork Tenderloin with Herbs and Garlic 24
Air Fryer Turkey Meatballs with Zucchini Noodles 24

Chapter 3 Fish and Seafood 25
Garlic and Herb Prawn Skewers 25
Crispy Prawn Cakes 25
Garlic Butter Prawn Skewers: 25
Air Fryer Salmon with Lemon and Dill 26
Garlic Parmesan Crusted Salmon 26
Cajun Tilapia 26
Grilled Lemon Herb Halibut 27
Lemon Garlic Baked Cod 27

Crispy salmon with lemon and dill 28
Air Fryer Mackerel Fillets 28
Air Fryer Trout with Lemon and Thyme ... 28
Air Fryer Tuna Steaks with Sesame Seeds ... 29
Air Fryer Blackened Salmon 29
Air Fryer Tuna Steaks with Lemon and Herbs
.... 29
Air Fryer Coconut Prawns 30
Air Fryer Battered Fish 30
Oat-Coated Fish 30
Air Fryer Fish Tempura 31
Air Fryer Lemon Garlic Salmon 31
Air Fryer Tuna Fish Cakes 32
Spicy Prawns: 32

Chapter 4 Poultry 33
Chicken Tenders 33
Air Fryer Turkey Breast 33
Air Fryer Duck Breast with Orange Glaze ... 33
Air Fryer Lemon and Herb Chicken Thighs 34
Air Fryer Lemon Garlic Turkey Breast 34
Air Fryer BBQ Chicken Wings 35
Air Fryer Chicken Satay 35
Air Fryer Chicken Satay Skewers 36
Air Fryer Turkey Burgers 36
Air Fryer Turkey Meatballs 37
Air Fryer Lemon Pepper Chicken 37
Honey Mustard Turkey Breast: 38
Crispy Duck Legs: 38
Airfryer Cajun Chicken Thighs 38
Airfryer Teriyaki Turkey Meatballs 39
Chicken Kiev 39
Air Fryer Teriyaki Chicken Thighs 40
Air Fryer Garlic Rosemary Turkey Breast ... 40

Chapter 5 Pork, Beef and Lamb 41
Air Fryer Pork Chops 41
Air Fryer Pork Tenderloin 41
Air Fryer Pork Belly Bites 41
Air Fryer Pork Chops with Mustard Crust ... 42
Honey Garlic Pork Chops 42
Air Fryer Pork Meatballs 42
Air Fryer Lamb Chops with Garlic and
Rosemary 43
Greek-Style Lamb Kabobs with Tzatziki ... 43
Air Fryer Lamb Kofta 44
Moroccan-Spiced Air Fryer Lamb Chops ... 44
Air Fryer Greek Lamb Chops 44
Air Fryer Moroccan Lamb Meatballs 45
Air Fryer Beef and Vegetable Kabobs 45
Air Fryer Beef Fajitas 45
Air Fryer Steak 46
Air Fryer Beef Jerky 46
Air Fryer Beef Kofta 47
Air Fryer Asian Beef Skewers 47

Chapter 6 Vegetable Recipes 48
Air Fryer Crispy Tofu 48
Roasted Cauliflower Steaks 48
Vegetable Fajitas 48
Air Fryer Sweet Potato Fries 49
Baked Sweet Potato Falafel 49
Courgette Fritters 50
Roasted Vegetables 50
Roasted Brussels Sprouts and Sweet Potatoes
.... 50
Stuffed Portobello Mushrooms 51
Air Fryer Veggie Burger 51
Air Fryer Tofu and Broccoli 52
Roasted Brussel Sprouts 52

Garlic Roasted Carrots 53
Air Fryer Asparagus 53
Air Fryer Green Beans 53
Air Fryer Veggie Skewers 54
Stuffed Courgettes 54
Airfryer Garlic Mushrooms 54
Airfryer Herb Roasted Potatoes 55
Airfryer Baked Potatoes 55
Airfryer Classic Potato Fries 55

Chapter 7 Snacks and Appetisers *56*
Airfryer Quinoa and Black Bean Cakes 56
Airfryer Crispy Kale 56
Airfryer Vegetable Pakoras 56
Porridge Bread 57
Fish Fingers................................. 57
Cauliflower Buffalo Wings 58
Air Fryer Mozzarella Sticks 58
Air Fryer Pita Chips 59
Crispy Brussels Sprouts Chips 59
Air Fryer Vegetable Spring Rolls: 60
Sweet Potato Tater Tots 60
Air Fryer Onion Rings: 61
Air Fryer Chicken Sliders 61
Air Fryer Sausage Rolls 62
Air Fryer 'Roasted' Peppers................... 62
Tuna Melt 62
Calzone 63
Halloumi Fries 63

Prosciutto Wrapped Asparagus 64
Crispy Chickpeas 64

Chapter 8 Desserts *65*
Air Fryer Chocolate Chip Cookies 65
Diabetic-Friendly Flapjacks 65
Diabetic-Friendly Shortbread 65
Apple and Mixed Berry Crumble (Diabetic-Friendly) 66
Diabetic-Friendly Chocolate Cake 66
Dried Strawberries 67
Blueberry Lemon Bars 67

Chapter 9 Bonus Recipes *68*
Banana Oat Cookies 68
Crab Cakes 68
Air Fryer Fish and Chips..................... 69
Air Fryer Ratatouille 69
Blueberry Muffins 70
Air Fryer Cinnamon Sugar Donut Holes ... 70
Granola 71
Breakfast Energy Balls 71
Air Fryer Diabetic-Friendly Soda Bread...... 72
Air Fryer Diabetic-Friendly Soda Bread...... 72
Air Fryer Cinnamon Sweet Potato Wedges 73
Cinnamon Roasted Almonds 73

30-Day Meal Plan *74*

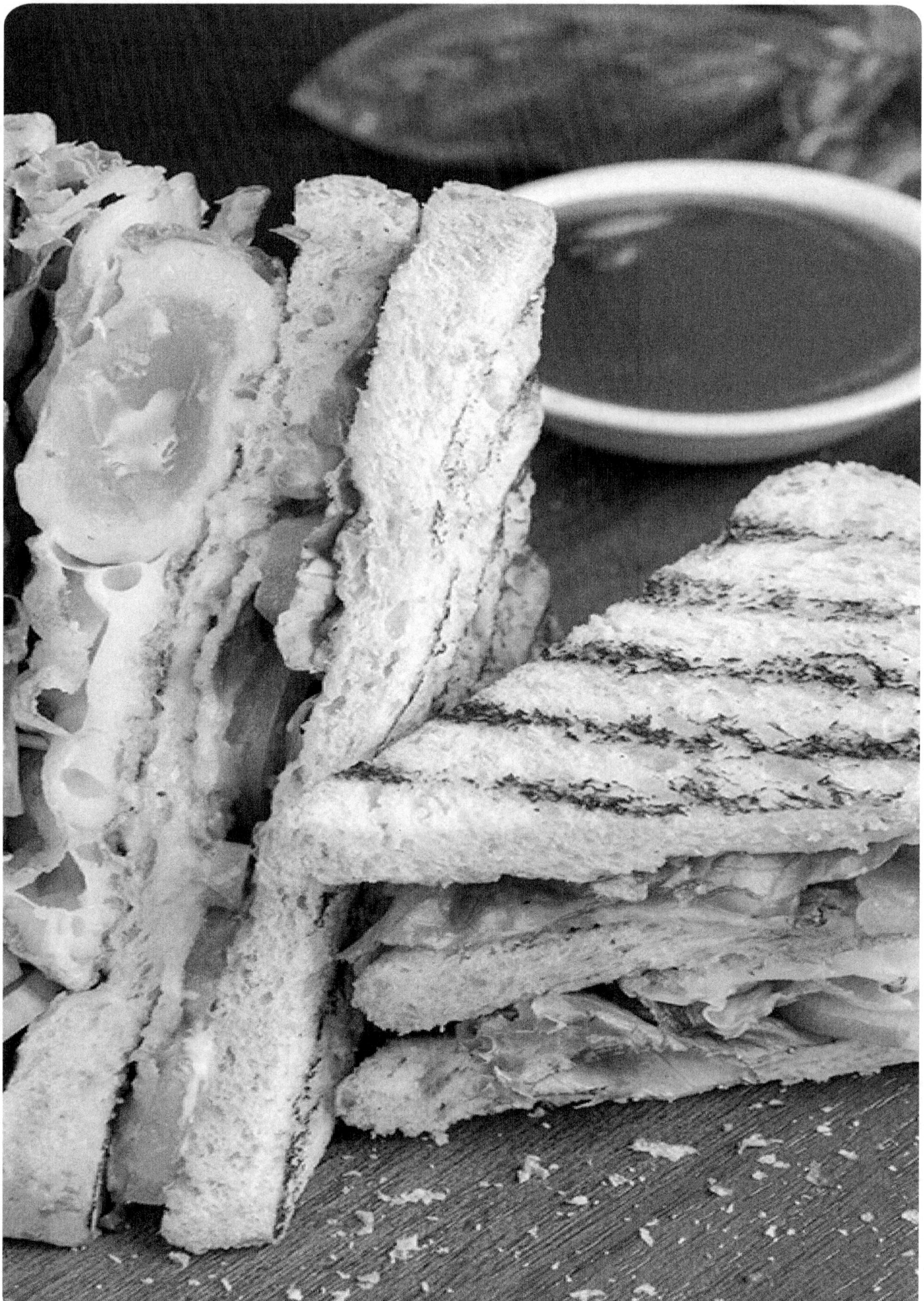

Introduction

Diabetes is a chronic condition that affects millions of people worldwide, and it can lead to serious health complications if not properly managed. Maintaining healthy blood sugar levels is crucial in diabetes management, and this often requires significant dietary modifications.

Many people with diabetes struggle with finding tasty and satisfying meal options that are also suitable for their dietary needs. This can lead to feelings of frustration and disappointment, which can make it difficult to stick to a healthy eating plan. However, using an air fryer can provide a solution to this problem. Air frying is a healthier cooking method that uses less oil than traditional frying, making it an excellent option for people with diabetes who want to enjoy delicious and crispy meals without compromising their health.

In this cookbook, we have carefully selected a variety of recipes that are not only healthy but also easy to prepare with an air fryer. We believe that eating healthy doesn't have to be boring, and we've included a range of flavorful dishes that will satisfy your taste buds while also supporting your diabetes management goals. Whether you're looking for breakfast, lunch, dinner, or snacks, this cookbook has something for everyone.

Living with diabetes can be challenging, and it often requires a lifestyle change to manage the disease. The use of air fryers has become increasingly popular in recent years, and it can be an excellent addition to a diabetic-friendly diet. In this cookbook, we aim to provide you with delicious and healthy recipes that can be easily made with an air fryer.

As a person living with diabetes, I understand the importance of maintaining a healthy and balanced diet. It can be challenging to find delicious and healthy recipes that are suitable for people with diabetes. That's why I am passionate about creating this cookbook, which offers a wide range of recipes that are both healthy and delicious.

Overall, our goal is to provide people with diabetes with a practical and accessible resource that can help them improve their health and well-being. We hope that this cookbook will inspire you to explore the world of air frying and discover new and exciting ways to enjoy healthy and delicious meals.

Chapter 1: Basics of Diabetes and Diabetic Diet

In this chapter, we will provide you with a comprehensive overview of diabetes, including the different types and causes of the disease. We will also discuss the components of a diabetic diet, the main goals and benefits of a diabetic diet, and what foods to avoid. This chapter aims to help you understand the importance of managing your diet when living with diabetes.

Chapter 2: Advantages of Using an Air Fryer in Healthy Living

Air fryers have become increasingly popular as a healthier alternative to traditional frying methods. In this chapter, we will discuss the benefits of using an air fryer in healthy living, specifically for people living with diabetes. We will cover what an air fryer is and how it works, the foods to avoid for an air fryer, and six benefits of using an air fryer. Additionally, we will provide tips for cooking in an air fryer for beginners.

Chapter 3: Benefits of Using the Recipes in the Book

In this chapter, we will discuss the benefits of using the recipes in the book, including how they can help manage diabetes. We will also highlight the nutritional value of the ingredients used in each recipe and how they can benefit your health. The recipes are designed to be easy to follow and provide delicious, healthy meals that can be made with an air fryer.

Overall, this cookbook aims to provide people living with diabetes with delicious and healthy recipes that can be easily made with an air fryer. By using the recipes in this book, you can take control of your diet and maintain a healthy and balanced lifestyle. We hope that this cookbook will be a valuable resource for you and your loved ones.

Chapter One

Diabetes is a chronic health condition that affects millions of people worldwide. It is a disease that affects how the body processes glucose or blood sugar. Glucose is an essential source of energy for our body, and insulin, a hormone produced by the pancreas, helps to regulate the amount of glucose in the bloodstream. In individuals with diabetes, the body cannot produce enough insulin, or it cannot effectively use the insulin it produces, leading to a buildup of glucose in the bloodstream. This can lead to a range of health complications and can have a significant impact on the overall quality of life.

Types of Diabetes

Type 1 and Type 2 diabetes are the most well-known forms of the disease, they have different causes and treatment approaches. Type 1 diabetes is an autoimmune condition in which the body's immune system attacks and destroys the cells in the pancreas that produce insulin. As a result, people with Type 1 diabetes must take insulin injections or use an insulin pump to manage their blood sugar levels. This type of diabetes is usually diagnosed in childhood or adolescence, but it can occur at any age.

Type 2 diabetes, on the other hand, is typically associated with lifestyle factors such as poor diet, lack of physical activity, and obesity. In Type 2 diabetes, the body becomes resistant to insulin or doesn't produce enough insulin to meet its needs. While Type 2 diabetes can often be managed through lifestyle changes such as diet and exercise, some people with this type of diabetes may also need to take medications such as metformin or insulin to keep their blood sugar levels under control.

Gestational diabetes is a type of diabetes that develops during pregnancy and usually goes away after the baby is born. However, women who have had gestational diabetes have an increased risk of developing Type 2 diabetes later in life. It is important for women with gestational diabetes to monitor their blood sugar levels closely during pregnancy to ensure the health of both mother and baby.

In addition to the three main types of diabetes (Type 1, Type 2, and gestational diabetes), there are other rarer forms of the disease. For example, monogenic diabetes is caused by a genetic mutation that affects insulin production, and it is often misdiagnosed as Type 1 or Type 2 diabetes. LADA (latent autoimmune diabetes in adults) is a form of Type 1 diabetes that occurs later in life and progresses more slowly than typical Type 1 diabetes. Other forms of diabetes include cystic fibrosis-related diabetes, which is caused by damage to the pancreas due to cystic fibrosis, and drug-induced diabetes, which can occur as a side effect of certain medications.

The Causes of Diabetes

The exact causes of diabetes are not fully understood, but it is believed that genetics, lifestyle factors, and environmental factors may all play a role. Some individuals may be genetically predisposed to diabetes, while others may develop diabetes due to lifestyle factors, such as poor diet and lack of physical activity. Environmental factors, such as exposure to certain toxins, may also increase the risk of developing diabetes.

The Components of a Diabetic Diet

Managing blood sugar levels is a critical part of managing diabetes, and a healthy diet is one of the most important components of diabetes management. A diabetic diet should include a variety of nutrient-dense foods, including vegetables, fruits, whole grains, lean proteins, and healthy fats. Foods that are high in sugar, saturated fats, and processed carbohydrates should be limited. Diabetics should aim to consume a balanced diet that provides a consistent source of energy throughout the day while avoiding spikes in blood sugar levels.

The Main Goals and Benefits of a Diabetic Diet

The main goals of a diabetic diet are to manage blood sugar levels, maintain a healthy weight, and prevent complications associated with diabetes. A healthy diet can help individuals with diabetes manage their blood sugar levels, reducing the risk of health complications, such as nerve damage, kidney disease, and vision problems. A diabetic diet can also help individuals maintain a healthy weight, reducing the risk of obesity-related health complications, such as heart disease and stroke.

What Foods to Avoid on a Diabetic Diet?

Individuals with diabetes should avoid foods that are high in sugar, saturated fats, and processed carbohydrates. Foods to avoid include sugary drinks, such as soft drinks and juices, processed snacks, such as chips and desserts, such as cakes and cookies. These foods can cause spikes in blood sugar levels and contribute to weight gain, making it harder to manage diabetes. Instead, individuals with diabetes should focus on consuming nutrient-dense foods that provide a consistent source of energy throughout the day, such as vegetables, fruits, whole grains, lean proteins, and healthy fats.

Chapter 2

Advantages of Using an Air Fryer in Healthy Living

Diabetes management requires a healthy and balanced diet that includes a variety of nutritious foods. However, cooking healthy meals can be challenging, especially for those who struggle with time management or have limited cooking skills. Fortunately, using an air fryer can make it easier to prepare healthy and diabetes-friendly meals.

Using an Air Fryer - Diabetes-Friendly Cooking Equipment

When it comes to managing diabetes, maintaining a healthy and balanced diet is crucial. An air fryer is a versatile kitchen appliance that can help you prepare delicious and healthy meals that are diabetes-friendly. Using an air fryer, you can reduce the amount of oil in your meals by up to 75%, making it a great option for people who need to reduce their fat and calorie intake.

The way an air fryer works is by circulating hot air around the food, which creates a crispy and golden exterior while keeping the inside moist and tender. This means that you can enjoy the crispy texture of fried foods without the added fat and calories

that come with traditional deep-frying methods.
In addition to reducing fat and calorie intake, using an air fryer can also help minimize the formation of harmful compounds that can occur when cooking with oil at high temperatures. These compounds, such as acrylamide and polycyclic aromatic hydrocarbons (PAHs), have been linked to an increased risk of certain types of cancer and other health problems. By using an air fryer instead of deep frying, you can significantly reduce your exposure to these harmful compounds, making it a healthier option overall.

Another advantage of using an air fryer is that it is a very versatile appliance that can be used to prepare a wide variety of dishes. From crispy chicken wings to roasted vegetables, an air fryer can handle a range of different foods, making it a great investment for anyone looking to diversify their cooking methods.

Foods to Avoid for an Air Fryer

While an air fryer is a great tool for cooking healthy and diabetes-friendly meals, there are some foods that are best avoided or limited when using this cooking method. One category of foods to be cautious of is high-fat foods. These include sausages, bacon, fatty cuts of meat, and other foods that are high in fat. When cooking these types of foods in an air fryer, the high fat content can cause the air fryer to smoke and create a burning smell, which can affect the flavor and quality of the food. To avoid this, it is recommended to trim excess fat from meats before cooking them in the air fryer, and to choose leaner cuts of meat whenever possible.

Another category of foods that should be used sparingly in an air fryer are those that are coated in batter or breadcrumbs. While these types of foods can be delicious when fried, they can become too dry and lose their crispy texture when cooked in an air fryer. To get around this, it is recommended to use a light coating of oil or egg wash before applying breadcrumbs or batter to foods, as this can help them to maintain their texture and flavor.

It is also important to note that some foods simply do not work well in an air fryer. For example, foods that are very moist or have a high water content, such as raw fruits and vegetables, are not recommended for air frying, as they may not cook evenly and can become soggy. In addition, foods that are very small or thin, such as shrimp or thinly sliced vegetables, may fall through the holes in the air fryer basket and not cook properly. To avoid these issues, it is recommended to use a grill or stovetop cooking method for these types of foods.

Chapter 3

Benefits of Using an Air Fryer

There are several benefits to using an air fryer in diabetes management and healthy living:

- **Reduced Fat Intake:** As mentioned earlier, using an air fryer can reduce the amount of fat in your meals by up to 75%, making it an ideal cooking method for those who need to manage their fat intake. Air fryers allow you to cook your favorite foods without the need for excessive amounts of oil or fat, making them an ideal tool for creating healthier versions of your favorite dishes. This can be especially helpful for those with diabetes, as a healthy diet is an essential component of managing the disease.

- **Quick and Easy Cooking:** Air fryers cook food faster than traditional cooking methods, making it an excellent option for busy individuals who need to prepare meals quickly.
- *Versatile Cooking*: Air fryers can be used to cook a variety of foods, from chicken and fish to vegetables and even desserts.
- *Reduced Risk of Harmful Compounds*: Using an air fryer can minimize the formation of harmful compounds that can occur when cooking with oil at high temperatures, making it a healthier cooking option.
- *No Need for Added Oil:* Air fryers do not require additional oil to cook food, reducing the amount of fat and calories in your meals. By eliminating the need for added oil, air fryers can help you prepare lower-calorie meals without sacrificing taste or texture. This can be particularly helpful for those who are trying to lose weight or maintain a healthy weight.
- *Easy to Clean*: Air fryers are generally easy to clean. Most models have dishwasher-safe components, making cleanup a breeze. This convenience can save you time and energy, allowing you to focus on other important tasks in your day-to-day life.

Tips for Cooking in an Air Fryer for Beginners

Using an air fryer may seem intimidating at first, but with these tips, you'll be a pro in no time:

Read the Instruction Manual: Before using your air fryer, be sure to read the instruction manual thoroughly to ensure you understand how to use it properly.

Preheat the Air Fryer: Preheating your air fryer can help ensure that your food cooks evenly and crisps up nicely.

Don't Overcrowd the Basket: Overcrowding the air fryer basket can prevent air from circulating properly and result in unevenly cooked food. Be sure to leave some space between each item.

Shake the Basket: Shaking the basket halfway through cooking can help ensure that your food cooks evenly on all sides.

Experiment with Seasonings: Air fryers are an excellent way to experiment with new flavour combinations and seasonings. Try adding different spices or herbs to your favorite foods to add an extra burst of flavor.

Clean Regularly: To ensure your air fryer lasts longer, it is essential to clean it regularly.

Conclusion

This cookbook offers a wide range of delicious and healthy recipes that can help you improve your health and manage your diabetes. By incorporating the recipes in this book into your daily diet, you can experience several benefits, including:

Improved blood sugar control: The recipes in this book are designed to be diabetes-friendly, with ingredients and cooking methods that can help you maintain stable blood sugar levels.

Increased variety in your diet: Following a diabetic diet can often be boring and repetitive, but this cookbook offers a range of diverse recipes that can add more excitement and variety to your meals.

Reduced risk of heart disease: Many of the recipes in this book use heart-healthy ingredients like lean protein, whole grains, and healthy fats, which can help you reduce your risk of heart disease and other related conditions.

Time-saving and convenient cooking: The air fryer is a versatile and convenient cooking tool that can help you prepare healthy meals quickly and easily. Using an air fryer can also help you reduce your use of oils and fats in cooking, which can be beneficial for diabetes management.

Delicious and satisfying meals: The recipes in this book are not only healthy, but also delicious and satisfying, so you won't feel like you're missing out on anything.

Lower calorie intake: Air fryers cook food by circulating hot air around it, resulting in crispy and flavorful food without the need for excess oil. This means that you can enjoy your favorite foods with fewer calories, which can help you manage your weight and improve your overall health.

By incorporating the recipes in this cookbook into your daily routine, you can experience these benefits and more. Whether you're looking to improve your diabetes management, eat healthier, or simply try out some new and delicious recipes, this cookbook has something for everyone. So go ahead and give these recipes a try – your body and taste buds will thank you!

In conclusion, this cookbook offers a variety of delicious and healthy recipes that are perfect for those living with diabetes. By using an air fryer, we've created meals that are lower in fat, calories, and harmful compounds, while still providing a satisfying and crispy texture. Whether you're a seasoned cook or new to using an air fryer, these recipes are simple to follow and sure to please. With this cookbook, we hope to inspire and support you in making healthy choices and enjoying the pleasures of food while managing your diabetes. So, let's get started with the recipes and enjoy tasty and diabetes-friendly meals together!

Chapter 1 Breakfast

Air Fryer Breakfast Burrito

Servings: 1

Cooking time: 10 minutes

Ingredients:
- 1 whole wheat tortilla
- 2 egg whites
- 45 g black beans, rinsed and drained
- 35 g chopped tomato
- 40 g chopped onion
- 30 g shredded cheddar cheese
- Salt and pepper to taste

Instructions:
1. Preheat the air fryer to 180°C.
2. In a bowl, whisk the egg whites, salt, and pepper until well combined.
3. Heat a non-stick pan over medium heat, spray with cooking spray, and pour in the egg mixture. Cook until set, then cut into small pieces.
4. Place the tortilla in the air fryer basket and add the cooked egg whites, black beans, tomato, onion, and cheese.
5. Roll up the tortilla and place it in the air fryer basket. Cook for 5 minutes or until the tortilla is crispy.

Per serving:
Calories: 322, Carbohydrates: 36g Protein: 27g Fat: 9g Cholesterol: 30mg Sodium: 707mg fibre: 15g

Air Fryer Cinnamon French Toast Sticks

Servings: 2

Cooking time: 10 minutes

Ingredients:
- 4 slices of whole wheat bread, cut into sticks
- 60ml unsweetened almond milk
- 1 large egg
- 1 teaspoon vanilla extract
- 1 teaspoon ground cinnamon
- 1/4 teaspoon nutmeg
- Cooking spray
- Sugar-free maple syrup for serving

Instructions:
1. Preheat the air fryer to 180°C.
2. In a mixing bowl, whisk together the almond milk, egg, vanilla extract, cinnamon, and nutmeg.
3. Dip each bread stick into the egg mixture, making sure it is coated on all sides.
4. Lightly coat the air fryer basket with cooking spray.
5. Place the bread sticks into the air fryer basket.
6. Cook for 5 minutes, then flip the sticks and cook for an additional 5 minutes or until the French
7. toast sticks are golden brown and crispy.

Serve with sugar-free maple syrup.

Note: If you prefer a sweeter French toast, you can sprinkle a little bit of sugar-free sweetener or cinnamon on top of the French toast sticks before serving.

Per serving(2 sticks):
Calories: 167,Carbohydrates: 22g Protein: 9g Fat: 5g Cholesterol: 186mg Sodium: 244mg Fiber: 4g

Air Fryer Omelette

Servings: 1

Cooking time: 8 minutes

Ingredients:
- 2 large eggs
- 35 g diced ham
- 40 g diced onion
- 40 g diced pepper
- 30 g shredded cheddar cheese
- Salt and pepper to taste

Instructions:
1. Preheat the air fryer to 175°C.
2. In a bowl, whisk the eggs, salt, and pepper until well combined.
3. Spray a small baking dish with cooking spray and pour in the egg mixture.
4. Add the ham, onion, pepper, and cheese on top of the egg mixture.
5. Place the baking dish in the air fryer basket and cook for 8 minutes or until the egg is set.

Per serving:
Calories: 310, Carbohydrates: 9g Protein: 28g Fat: 19g Cholesterol: 386mg Sodium: 867mg fibre: 1g

Air Fryer Breakfast Hash

Servings: 1

Cooking time: 20 minutes

Ingredients:
- 1 small sweet potato (130g), peeled and diced
- 2 slices bacon, diced
- 40 g diced onion
- 40 g diced pepper
- 1/4 tsp garlic powder
- 1/4 tsp paprika
- Salt and pepper to taste
- 1 large egg

Instructions:
1. Preheat the air fryer to 195°C.
2. In a bowl, mix the sweet potato, bacon, onion, pepper, garlic powder, paprika, salt, and pepper until well combined.
3. Place the mixture in the air fryer basket and cook for 15 minutes, stirring once halfway through.
4. Crack the egg on top of the sweet potato mixture, season with salt and pepper, and cook for an additional 5 minutes or until the egg is set.

Per serving:
Calories: 292, Carbohydrates: 24g Protein: 14g Fat: 17g Cholesterol: 229mg Sodium: 476mg fibre: 4g

Note: You can add more vegetables, like mushrooms or spinach, to this hash if you like. Just adjust the Cooking time accordingly.

Air Fryer Cinnamon French Toast

Servings: 1

Cooking time: 10 minutes

Ingredients:
- 2 slices of whole wheat bread
- 1 egg
- 60 ml unsweetened almond milk
- 1/2 tsp ground cinnamon
- 1/4 tsp vanilla extract
- Cooking spray
- Sugar-free maple syrup, for serving (optional)

Instructions:
1. Preheat the air fryer to 180°C.
2. In a bowl, whisk the egg, almond milk,

ground cinnamon, and vanilla extract until well combined.
3. Dip each slice of bread into the egg mixture until fully coated.
4. Spray the air fryer basket with cooking spray and place the bread slices in the basket.
5. Cook for 5 minutes, then flip the bread slices and cook for an additional 5 minutes.
6. Serve with sugar-free maple syrup, if desired.

Per serving:

Calories: 231, Carbohydrates: 25g Protein: 15g Fat: 8g Cholesterol: 186mg Sodium: 351mg fibre: 5g

Air Fryer Egg and Veggie Muffins

Servings: 4

Cooking time: 20 minutes

Ingredients:

- 200g egg whites
- 100g diced courgette
- 50g diced red pepper
- 50g diced yellow onion
- 50g shredded low-fat cheddar cheese
- Salt and pepper to taste
- Cooking spray

Instructions:

1. Preheat the air fryer to 180°C.
2. In a bowl, whisk the egg whites and season with salt and pepper.
3. Add the courgette, pepper, onion, and cheese to the egg mixture and stir to combine.
4. Spray a silicone muffin tin with cooking spray and pour in the egg mixture, filling each mold about 2/3 full.
5. Place the muffin tin in the air fryer basket and cook for 15-20 minutes or until the egg muffins are set and slightly golden on top.
6. Remove from the air fryer and let cool for a few minutes before removing the muffins from the tin.
7. Serve warm or at room temperature.

Per serving (1 muffin):

Calories: 62, Carbohydrates: 2g Protein: 10g Fat: 2g Cholesterol: 5mg Sodium: 170mg fibre: 0g

Air Fryer Sweet Potato Toast

Servings: 2

Cooking time: 10 minutes

Ingredients:

- 200g sweet potato, sliced into ½ cm rounds
- 1 tbsp olive oil
- Salt and pepper to taste
- Toppings of your choice, such as avocado, sliced tomatoes, feta cheese, or fried eggs

Instructions:

1. Preheat the air fryer to 200°C.
2. Toss the sweet potato rounds with olive oil, salt, and pepper.
3. Place the sweet potato rounds in a single layer in the air fryer basket.
4. Cook for 8-10 minutes or until the sweet potato is tender and slightly browned on the edges.
5. Remove from the air fryer and top with your desired toppings.
6. Serve hot.

Per serving (1/2 recipe without toppings):

Calories: 89, Carbohydrates: 13g Protein: 1g Fat: 4g Cholesterol: 0mg Sodium: 44mg fibre: 2g

Air Fryer Blueberry Muffins

Servings: 4

Cooking time: 20 minutes

Ingredients:
- 100g almond flour
- 50g coconut flour
- 2 tbsp granulated sweetener of your choice
- 1 tsp baking powder
- 1/4 tsp salt
- 100g unsweetened almond milk
- 50g unsweetened applesauce
- 2 large eggs
- 1 tsp vanilla extract
- 50g fresh blueberries

Instructions:
1. Preheat the air fryer to 180°C.
2. In a mixing bowl, whisk together the almond flour, coconut flour, sweetener, baking powder, and salt.
3. In another bowl, whisk together the almond milk, applesauce, eggs, and vanilla extract.
4. Add the wet Ingredients to the dry Ingredients and stir until well combined.
5. Fold in the blueberries.
6. Spray a silicone muffin tin with cooking spray and pour in the batter, filling each mold about 2/3 full.
7. Place the muffin tin in the air fryer basket and cook for 15-20 minutes or until the muffins are set and slightly golden on top.
8. Remove from the air fryer and let cool for a few minutes before removing the muffins from the tin.
9. Serve warm or at room temperature.

Per serving (1 muffin):
Calories: 153, Carbohydrates: 9g Protein: 7g Fat: 11g Cholesterol: 93mg Sodium: 179mg fibre: 5g

Air Fryer French Toast Sticks

Servings: 2

Cooking time: 10 minutes

Ingredients:
- 2 slices low-carb bread, cut into strips
- 2 large eggs
- 50g unsweetened almond milk
- 1/2 tsp vanilla extract
- 1/2 tsp ground cinnamon
- 1/4 tsp nutmeg
- 2 tbsp granulated sweetener of your choice
- Cooking spray

Instructions:
1. Preheat the air fryer to 190°C.
2. In a mixing bowl, whisk together the eggs, almond milk, vanilla extract, cinnamon, nutmeg, and sweetener.
3. Dip each bread strip into the egg mixture, making sure to coat both sides well.
4. Spray the air fryer basket with cooking spray and place the bread strips in a single layer.
5. Cook for 6-8 minutes or until the French toast sticks are golden brown and crispy.
6. Serve hot with sugar-free syrup or fresh berries.

Per serving (1/2 recipe):
Calories: 126, Carbohydrates: 8g Protein: 9g Fat: 6g Cholesterol: 186mg Sodium: 245mg fibre: 4g

Air Fryer Breakfast Sausage Patties

Servings: 4

Cooking time: 10 minutes

Ingredients:
- 250g turkey mince
- 1 tsp dried sage
- 1/2 tsp garlic powder

- 1/2 tsp onion powder
- Salt and pepper to taste
- Cooking spray

Instructions:

1. Preheat the air fryer to 200°C.
2. In a mixing bowl, combine the turkey mince, sage, garlic powder, onion powder, salt, and pepper.
3. Form the sausage mixture into 8 equal-sized patties.
4. Spray the air fryer basket with cooking spray and place the sausage patties in a single layer.
5. Cook for 5-7 minutes or until the sausage patties are browned and cooked through.
6. Remove from the air fryer and let cool for a few minutes before serving.

Per serving (2 patties):

Calories: 149, Carbohydrates: 1g Protein: 18g Fat: 8g Cholesterol: 82mg Sodium: 404mg fibre: 0g

Air Fryer Cinnamon Apple Chips

Servings: 2

Cooking time: 15 minutes

Ingredients:

- 2 medium apples, cored and thinly sliced
- 1 tsp ground cinnamon
- 1 tbsp granulated sweetener of your choice

Instructions:

1. Preheat the air fryer to 150°C.
2. In a mixing bowl, toss the apple slices with cinnamon and sweetener until well coated.
3. Place the apple slices in the air fryer basket in a single layer.
4. Cook for 10-12 minutes or until the apple chips are crispy and golden brown.
5. Remove from the air fryer and let cool for a few minutes before serving.

Per serving:

Calories: 69, Carbohydrates: 19g Protein: 0g Fat: 0g Cholesterol: 0mg Sodium: 0mg fibre: 3g

Air Fryer Breakfast Stuffed Peppers

Servings: 2

Cooking time: 20 minutes

Ingredients:

- 2 peppers, halved and seeded
- 150g breakfast sausage, cooked and crumbled
- 2 large eggs, beaten
- 50g shredded cheddar cheese
- Salt and pepper to taste
- Cooking spray

Instructions:

1. Preheat the air fryer to 180°C.
2. In a mixing bowl, combine the cooked breakfast sausage, beaten eggs, shredded cheese, salt, and pepper.
3. Stuff each pepper half with the sausage mixture.
4. Spray the air fryer basket with cooking spray and place the stuffed bell peppers in a single layer.
5. Cook for 12-15 minutes or until the eggs are set and the peppers are tender.
6. Serve hot.

Per serving:

Calories: 246, Carbohydrates: 8g Protein: 18g Fat: 16g Cholesterol: 226mg Sodium: 481mg fibre: 2g

Air Fryer Banana Oatmeal Muffins

Servings: 6

Cooking time: 20 minutes

Ingredients:
- 2 ripe bananas, mashed
- 2 large eggs, beaten
- 80g rolled oats
- 1 tsp baking powder
- 1 tsp ground cinnamon
- 1/2 tsp vanilla extract
- 1/4 tsp salt
- 1 tbsp granulated sweetener of your choice
- Cooking spray

Instructions:
1. Preheat the air fryer to 180°C..
2. In a mixing bowl, combine the mashed bananas, beaten eggs, rolled oats, baking powder, cinnamon, vanilla extract, salt, and sweetener.
3. Mix until well combined.
4. Divide the mixture evenly among 6 silicone muffin cups or spray the air fryer basket with cooking spray and pour the mixture into 6 muffin cups.
5. Place the muffin cups in the air fryer basket and cook for 15-20 minutes or until a toothpick inserted into the center of a muffin comes out clean.
6. Remove from the air fryer and let cool for a few minutes before serving.

Per serving:
Calories: 92, Carbohydrates: 15g Protein: 3g Fat: 3g Cholesterol: 62mg Sodium: 181mg fibre: 2g

Air Fryer Turkey and Spinach Frittata

Servings: 4

Cooking time: 25 minutes

Ingredients:
- 8 large eggs, beaten
- 200g turkey mince
- 100g fresh baby spinach, chopped
- 60 g shredded mozzarella cheese
- 25 g grated Parmesan cheese
- 1 tsp garlic powder
- 1 tsp onion powder
- Salt and pepper to taste
- Cooking spray

Instructions:
1. Preheat the air fryer to 180°C.
2. In a frying pan over medium heat, cook the turkey mince until browned and cooked through.
3. Add the chopped spinach to the frying pan and cook for another 1-2 minutes or until wilted.
4. In a mixing bowl, whisk the eggs with garlic powder, onion powder, salt, and pepper.
5. Stir in the cooked turkey and spinach, shredded mozzarella cheese, and grated Parmesan cheese.
6. Spray the air fryer basket with cooking spray and pour the egg mixture into the basket.
7. Cook for 20-25 minutes or until the frittata is set and the top is golden brown.
8. Remove from the air fryer and let cool for a few minutes before serving.

Per serving:
Calories: 242, Carbohydrates: 2g Protein: 24g Fat: 15g Cholesterol: 435mg Sodium: 397mg fibre: 0g

Air Fryer Blueberry Scones

Servings: 4

Cooking time: 15 minutes

Ingredients:
- 80g almond flour
- 40g coconut flour
- 10 g granulated sweetener of your choice
- 1 tsp baking powder
- 1/4 tsp salt
- 2 large eggs, beaten
- 2 tbsp coconut oil, melted
- 75 g fresh blueberries
- Cooking spray

Instructions:
1. Preheat the air fryer to 180°C.
2. In a mixing bowl, combine the almond flour, coconut flour, sweetener, baking powder, and salt.
3. Add the beaten eggs and melted coconut oil to the mixing bowl and mix until well combined.
4. Gently fold in the fresh blueberries.
5. Spray the air fryer basket with cooking spray and scoop the scone dough into 4 even portions onto the basket.
6. Cook for 12-15 minutes or until the scones are golden brown and cooked through.
7. Remove from the air fryer and let cool for a few minutes before serving.

Per serving:
Calories: 221, Carbohydrates: 10g Protein: 7g Fat: 18g Cholesterol: 124mg Sodium: 239mg fibre: 4g

Air Fryer Sweet Potato Hash Browns

Servings: 4

Cooking time: 20 minutes

Ingredients:
- 500g sweet potatoes, peeled and shredded
- 1 small onion, finely chopped
- 2 cloves garlic, minced
- 2 tbsp coconut oil, melted
- 1 tsp smoked paprika
- 1/2 tsp dried thyme
- Salt and pepper to taste
- Cooking spray

Instructions:
1. Preheat the air fryer to 180°C.
2. In a mixing bowl, combine the shredded sweet potatoes, finely chopped onion, minced garlic, melted coconut oil, smoked paprika, dried thyme, salt, and pepper.
3. Mix until well combined.
4. Spray the air fryer basket with cooking spray and pour the sweet potato mixture into the basket.
5. Cook for 15-20 minutes or until the hash browns are crispy and cooked through, stirring occasionally to prevent sticking.
6. Remove from the air fryer and let cool for a few minutes before serving.

Per serving:
Calories: 143, Carbohydrates: 21g Protein: 2g Fat: 6g Cholesterol: 0mg Sodium: 94mg fibre: 3g

Air Fryer Greek Omelette

Servings: 2

Cooking time: 15 minutes

Ingredients:

- 100g cherry tomatoes, halved
- 1 small red onion, finely chopped
- 50g baby spinach leaves
- 4 large eggs
- 30 g crumbled feta cheese
- 1/2 tsp dried oregano
- Salt and pepper to taste
- Cooking spray

Instructions:

1. Preheat the air fryer to 180°C.
2. In a mixing bowl, whisk together the eggs, crumbled feta cheese, dried oregano, salt, and pepper.
3. Spray the air fryer basket with cooking spray and pour the egg mixture into the basket.
4. Add the halved cherry tomatoes, finely chopped red onion, and baby spinach leaves on top of the egg mixture.
5. Cook for 10-12 minutes or until the omelette is set and cooked through.
6. Remove from the air fryer and let cool for a few minutes before serving.

Per serving:

Calories: 192, Carbohydrates: 6g Protein: 14g Fat: 13g Cholesterol: 347mg Sodium: 323mg fibre: 2g

Air Fryer Coconut Flour Pancakes

Servings: 4

Cooking time: 10 minutes

Ingredients:

- 50g coconut flour
- 1/4 tsp baking soda
- 1/4 tsp salt
- 4 large eggs
- 60 ml unsweetened almond milk
- 2 tbsp coconut oil, melted
- 1 tsp vanilla extract
- 1-2 tbsp sweetener of your choice
- Cooking spray
- Fresh berries, for serving

Instructions:

1. Preheat the air fryer to 180°C.
2. In a mixing bowl, whisk together the coconut flour, baking soda, and salt.
3. In another mixing bowl, whisk together the eggs, unsweetened almond milk, melted coconut oil, vanilla extract, and sweetener until well combined.
4. Pour the wet Ingredients into the dry Ingredients and mix until smooth.
5. Spray the air fryer basket with cooking spray and pour 1/4 cup of the pancake batter into the basket, leaving space between each pancake.
6. Cook the pancakes for 3-4 minutes or until bubbles form on the surface and the edges start to turn golden brown.
7. Flip the pancakes and cook for an additional 2-3 minutes or until they are cooked through.
8. Repeat with the remaining pancake batter, spraying the basket with cooking spray between batches.
9. Serve with fresh berries.

Per serving:

Calories: 129, Carbohydrates: 6g Protein: 6g Fat: 9g Cholesterol: 164mg Sodium: 198mg fibre: 3g

Air Fryer Apple Cinnamon Oatmeal

Servings: 1

Cooking time: 12 minutes

Ingredients:
- 40g rolled oats
- 120 ml unsweetened almond milk
- 75 g chopped apple (any variety)
- 1 teaspoon unsweetened applesauce
- 1/2 teaspoon cinnamon
- 1/4 teaspoonl vanilla extract
- 1/4 teaspoon salt

Instructions:
1. Preheat the air fryer to 180°C.
2. In a mixing bowl, combine the rolled oats, almond milk, chopped apple, applesauce, cinnamon, vanilla extract, and salt.
3. Mix well to combine.
4. Lightly coat a small oven-safe ramekin or baking dish with cooking spray.
5. Pour the oatmeal mixture into the ramekin or dish.
6. Place the ramekin or dish into the air fryer basket.
7. Cook for 12 minutes or until the oatmeal is cooked and the top is golden brown.
8. Remove from the air fryer and let cool for a few minutes before serving.

Per serving:
Calories: 255,Carbohydrates: 43g Protein: 8g Fat: 6g Cholesterol: 0mg Sodium: 418mg Fiber: 7g

Air Fryer Baked Oats

Servings: 2

Cooking time: 20 minutes

Ingredients:
- 50g rolled oats
- 120ml unsweetened almond milk
- 60g unsweetened applesauce
- 15g chia seeds
- 10g honey or sugar substitute
- 2g ground cinnamon

Instructions:
1. Preheat the air fryer to 180°C.
2. In a mixing bowl, combine the rolled oats, almond milk, applesauce, chia seeds, honey (or sugar substitute), and cinnamon. Mix well to combine.
3. Divide the mixture evenly into 2 greased ramekins or oven-safe dishes.
4. Place the ramekins into the air fryer and cook for 20 minutes, or until the oats are set and the top is golden brown.
5. Remove from the air fryer and allow to cool for a few minutes before serving. Enjoy!

Per serving:
Calories: 151, Carbohydrates: 22g, Fats: 4g, Protein: 5g, Cholesterol: 0mg, Sodium: 83mg fibre: 6g

Air Fryer Breakfast Quiche

Servings: 4

Cooking time: 25 minutes

Ingredients:
- 200g large eggs
- 60ml unsweetened almond milk
- 30g chopped pepper
- 30g chopped onion
- 30g chopped spinach
- 30g shredded cheddar cheese
- Salt and pepper to taste

Instructions:
1. Preheat the air fryer to 180°C.
2. In a mixing bowl, whisk together the eggs and almond milk until well combined.
3. Add the chopped pepper, onion, spinach, shredded cheddar cheese, salt, and pepper to the bowl. Mix well to combine.
4. Pour the mixture into a greased baking dish that fits inside your air fryer basket.
5. Place the dish into the air fryer and cook for 25 minutes, or until the quiche is set and the top is golden brown.
6. Remove from the air fryer and allow to cool for a few minutes before slicing and serving. Enjoy!

Per serving:
Calories: 125, Carbohydrates: 2g, Fats: 9g, Protein: 9g, Cholesterol: 191mg, Sodium: 174mg fibre: 0.5g

Air Fryer Breakfast Burritos

Servings: 2

Cooking time: 10 minutes

Ingredients:
- 2 large eggs, beaten
- 40g chopped bell pepper (any color)
- 40g chopped onion
- 2 tablespoons chopped fresh cilantro
- 0.6g ground cumin
- Salt and pepper to taste
- 2 whole wheat tortillas
- 30g shredded reduced-fat cheddar cheese
- Cooking spray

Instructions:
1. Preheat the air fryer to 180°C.
2. In a mixing bowl, whisk together the beaten eggs, chopped bell pepper, chopped onion, chopped cilantro, ground cumin, salt, and pepper.
3. Lightly coat a small oven-safe baking dish or ramekin with cooking spray.
4. Pour the egg mixture into the dish or ramekin.
5. Place the dish or ramekin into the air fryer basket. Cook for 10 minutes or until the eggs are set.
6. Remove from the air fryer and let cool for a few minutes. Warm the tortillas in the microwave or oven.
7. Divide the egg mixture and shredded cheese evenly between the two tortillas.
8. Roll up the tortillas into burritos.
9. Lightly coat the air fryer basket with cooking spray.
10. Place the burritos into the air fryer basket. Cook for 5-7 minutes or until the burritos are heated through and crispy on the outside.
11. Serve warm.

Per serving:
Calories: 259, Carbohydrates: 26g, Fats: 9g, Protein: 16g, Cholesterol: 194mg, Sodium: 464mg fibre: 5g

Chapter 2 Main Recipes

Chicken Breasts

Serves: 2
Cooking time: 20 minutes

Ingredients:
- 2 boneless, skinless chicken breasts
- 1 tbsp olive oil
- Salt and pepper, to taste

Instructions:
1. Preheat the air fryer to 190°C.
2. Brush the chicken breasts with olive oil and season with salt and pepper.
3. Place the chicken in the air fryer basket and cook for 18-20 minutes, flipping once halfway through cooking.
4. Check the internal temperature of the chicken with a meat thermometer. It should read 74°C.
5. Serve hot.

Per serving:
Calories: 200 fat:7g , carbohydrates:0g, protein:31g, sodium:380mg , fibre:0g .

Air Fryer Fish Fillets

Serves: 2
Cooking time: 12 minutes

Ingredients:
- 2 tilapia fillets
- 1 tbsp olive oil
- 1 tsp paprika
- 1/2 tsp garlic powder
- Salt and pepper, to taste

Instructions:
1. Preheat the air fryer to 190°C.
2. Brush the fish fillets with olive oil and season with paprika, garlic powder, salt, and pepper.
3. Place the fish in the air fryer basket and cook for 10-12 minutes, flipping once halfway through cooking.
4. Check the internal temperature of the fish with a meat thermometer. It should read 63°C.
5. Serve hot.

Per serving:
Calories: 259, Carbohydrates: 20g, Fats: 0g, Protein: 20g,Sodium: 170mg fibre: 0g

Turkey and Vegetable Skillet

Serves: 4
Cooking time: 15 minutes

Ingredients:
- 1 tablespoon olive oil
- 450g ground turkey
- 1 medium onion, chopped
- 2 cloves garlic, minced
- 2 medium zucchinis, chopped
- 1 red bell pepper, chopped
- 1 teaspoon dried oregano
- 1/2 teaspoon salt
- 1/4 teaspoon black pepper

Instructions:
1. Heat the olive oil in a large skillet over medium-high heat.
2. Add the ground turkey and cook, breaking it up with a wooden spoon, for 5-6 minutes or until browned and cooked through.
3. Add the chopped onion and minced garlic to the skillet.
4. Cook for 2-3 minutes or until the onion is translucent and the garlic is fragrant.
5. Add the chopped zucchinis, chopped red bell pepper, oregano, salt, and black pepper to the skillet.

6. Stir to combine.
7. Cover the skillet and cook for 8-10 minutes or until the vegetables are tender.
8. Serve hot.

Per serving:

Calories: 226, Carbohydrates: 8g, Fats: 9g, Protein: 29g, Sodium: 392mg fibre: 2g

Air Fryer Salmon

Serves: 2

Cooking time: 12 minutes

Ingredients:

- 2 salmon fillets
- 1 tbsp olive oil
- Salt and pepper, to taste

Instructions:

1. Preheat the air fryer to 200°C.
2. Brush the salmon fillets with olive oil and season with salt and pepper.
3. Place the salmon in the air fryer basket and cook for 10-12 minutes, depending on the thickness of the fillets.
4. Check the internal temperature of the salmon with a meat thermometer. It should read 63°C.
5. Serve hot.

Per serving:

Calories: 250, Carbohydrates: 0g, Fats: 15g, Protein: 26g, Sodium: 380mg fibre: 0g

Air Fryer Turkey Burgers

Serves: 4

Cooking time: 15 minutes

Ingredients:

- 455 g turkey mince
- 1 egg
- 50 g almond flour
- 1/2 tsp garlic powder
- Salt and pepper, to taste

Instructions:

1. Preheat the air fryer to 200°C.
2. In a mixing bowl, combine turkey mince, egg, almond flour, garlic powder, salt, and pepper. Mix well.
3. Form the mixture into 4 patties.
4. Place the patties in the air fryer basket and cook for 12-15 minutes, flipping once halfway through cooking.
5. Check the internal temperature of the burgers with a meat thermometer. It should read 74°C.
6. Serve hot.

Per serving:

Calories: 260, Carbohydrates: 4g, Fats: 15g, Protein: 27g, Sodium: 190mg fibre: 2g

Air Fryer Pork Chops

Serves: 2

Cooking time: 18 minutes

Ingredients:

- 2 boneless pork chops
- 50 g almond flour
- 1/2 tsp paprika
- 1/2 tsp garlic powder
- Salt and pepper, to taste

Instructions:

1. Preheat the air fryer to 200°C.
2. In a mixing bowl, combine almond flour, paprika, garlic powder, salt, and pepper.
3. Dredge the pork chops in the mixture, making sure they are fully coated.
4. Place the pork chops in the air fryer basket and cook for 16-18 minutes, flipping once halfway through cooking.
5. Check the internal temperature of the pork chops with a meat thermometer. It should read 63°C.
6. Serve hot.

Per serving:
Calories: 260, Carbohydrates:4g, Fats: 15g, Protein: 27g,Sodium: 190mg fibre: 2g

Air Fryer Beef Kabobs

Serves: 4

Cooking time: 15 minutes

Ingredients:
- 455 g beef sirloin, cut into cubes
- 1 red pepper, cut into squares
- 1 green pepper, cut into squares
- 1 onion, cut into squares
- 2 tbsp olive oil
- 1 tsp paprika
- 1/2 tsp garlic powder
- Salt and pepper, to taste

Instructions:
1. Preheat the air fryer to 200°C.
2. In a mixing bowl, combine beef cubes, redl pepper, green pepper, onion, olive oil, paprika, garlic powder, salt, and pepper.
3. Thread the beef and vegetables onto skewers.
4. Place the skewers in the air fryer basket and cook for 12-15 minutes, flipping once halfway through cooking.
5. Check the internal temperature of the beef with a meat thermometer. It should read 63°C for medium-rare.
6. Serve hot.

Per serving:
Calories: 230, Carbohydrates:6g, Fats: 12g, Protein: 24g,Sodium: 210mg fibre: 2g

Air Fryer Chicken Thighs

Serves: 2

Cooking time: 20 minutes

Ingredients:
- 4 bone-in, skin-on chicken thighs
- 1 tbsp olive oil
- Salt and pepper, to taste

Instructions:
1. Preheat the air fryer to 190°C.
2. Brush the chicken thighs with olive oil and season with salt and pepper.
3. Place the chicken in the air fryer basket and cook for 18-20 minutes, flipping once halfway through cooking.
4. Check the internal temperature of the chicken with a meat thermometer. It should read 74°C.
5. Serve hot.

Per serving:
Calories: 280, Carbohydrates:22g, Fats: 20g, Protein: 24g,Sodium: 130mg fibre: 0g

Air Fryer Chicken Parmesan

Servings: 4

Cooking time: 20 minutes

Ingredients:
- 500g boneless, skinless chicken breasts
- 60g almond flour
- 60g grated Parmesan cheese
- 2g garlic powder
- 2g onion powder
- 2g dried basil
- 2g dried oregano
- Salt and pepper to taste
- 1 large egg, beaten
- 60g sugar-free tomato sauce
- 60g shredded mozzarella cheese
- Fresh basil, chopped, for garnish

Instructions:
1. Preheat the air fryer to 190°C.
2. Cut the chicken breasts into thin cutlets.
3. In a mixing bowl, combine the almond flour, grated Parmesan cheese, garlic powder, onion powder, dried basil, dried oregano, salt, and

pepper. Mix well.
4. Dip each chicken cutlet into the beaten egg, then coat it in the almond flour mixture. Place the coated chicken onto the air fryer basket or tray.
5. Air fry the chicken for 8 minutes. Flip the chicken over, then air fry for another 5-7 minutes, or until cooked through and crispy.
6. Spoon the tomato sauce onto each chicken cutlet, then sprinkle with shredded mozzarella cheese.
7. Air fry for another 2-3 minutes, or until the cheese is melted and bubbly.
8. Garnish with fresh basil, if desired, then serve and enjoy!

Per serving:
Calories: 329, Carbohydrates: 6g, Fats: 13g, Protein: 47g, Cholesterol: 165mg, Sodium: 606mg, fibre: 1g

Salmon with Lemon-Dill Sauce

Servings: 4
Cooking time: 15 minutes

Ingredients:
- 500g salmon fillets
- 2g garlic powder
- 2g onion powder
- 2g dried dill weed
- Salt and pepper to taste
- 1 large lemon, sliced
- 60g plain Greek yogurt
- 15g fresh dill, chopped
- 5g lemon zest

Instructions:
1. Preheat the air fryer to 190°C.
2. Cut the salmon fillets into 4 portions.
3. In a small bowl, mix together the garlic powder, onion powder, dried dill weed, salt, and pepper.
4. Season the salmon fillets with the seasoning mixture.
5. Place the salmon fillets onto the air fryer basket or tray, skin side down.
6. Arrange the lemon slices on top of the salmon fillets.
7. Air fry the salmon for 10-12 minutes, or until cooked through and flaky.
8. While the salmon is cooking, prepare the lemon-dill sauce. In a small mixing bowl, combine the Greek yogurt, fresh dill, and lemon zest. Mix well.
9. Serve the salmon with the lemon-dill sauce on top.

Per serving:
Calories: 269, Carbohydrates: 4g, Fats: 14g, Protein: 31g, Sodium: 81mg fibre: 1g

Air Fryer Beef and Broccoli Stir-Fry

Servings: 4
Cooking time: 20 minutes

Ingredients:
- 500g beef sirloin, thinly sliced
- 10g cornflour
- 5g soy sauce
- 2g garlic powder
- 2g ground ginger
- 1g black pepper
- 5g olive oil
- 400g broccoli florets
- 50g sliced onion
- 5g minced garlic
- 20g low-sodium soy sauce
- 10g brown sugar substitute
- 5g sesame oil

Instructions:
1. Preheat the air fryer to 190°C.
2. In a bowl, mix the beef sirloin, cornflour, soy sauce, garlic powder, ginger, and black pepper.

3. Drizzle the olive oil on top of the beef and mix well to coat.
4. Place the beef in the air fryer basket or tray, in a single layer. Air fry for 8-10 minutes, or until cooked through and crispy.
5. In the meantime, prepare the broccoli florets by washing and drying them.
6. In a mixing bowl, combine the broccoli florets, sliced onion, minced garlic, low-sodium soy sauce, and brown sugar substitute. Mix well to coat the vegetables.
7. After the beef is done, remove it from the air fryer basket and set it aside.
8. Place the broccoli mixture in the air fryer basket and air fry for 8-10 minutes, or until the broccoli is tender and slightly crispy.
9. Once the broccoli is done, add the cooked beef to the air fryer basket with the broccoli and mix well.
10. Drizzle the sesame oil over the beef and broccoli mixture and mix well.
11. Air fry for an additional 2-3 minutes to allow the flavours to meld together.
12. Serve the beef and broccoli stir-fry hot.

Per serving:

Calories: 254, Carbohydrates: 12g, Fats: 12g, Protein: 26g, Cholesterol: 69mg, Sodium: 443mg, fibre: 3g

Air Fryer Lemon Garlic Chicken

Servings: 4

Cooking time: 25 minutes

Ingredients:

- 4 chicken breasts (about 600g), boneless and skinless
- 10g olive oil
- 3g minced garlic
- 1tsp dried oregano
- 1tsp dried basil
- 1tsp paprika
- ½ tsp salt
- ½ tsp black pepper
- 1 lemon, sliced

Instructions:

1. Preheat the air fryer to 190°C.
2. Rinse the chicken breasts and pat dry with a paper towel.
3. In a small bowl, mix together the olive oil, minced garlic, oregano, basil, paprika, salt, and black pepper.
4. Brush the mixture over both sides of the chicken breasts.
5. Place the chicken breasts in the air fryer basket or tray.
6. Top each chicken breast with a slice of lemon.
7. Air fry for 20-25 minutes, or until the chicken is cooked through and the internal temperature reaches 74°C.
8. Serve the lemon garlic chicken hot with your favourite side dish.

Per serving:

Calories: 202, Carbohydrates: 2g, Fats: 7g, Protein: 33g, Cholesterol: 96mg, Sodium: 436mg, fibre: 1g

Air Fryer Fish Tacos with Mango Salsa

Servings: 4

Cooking time: 20 minutes

Ingredients:

- 500g white fish fillets (such as tilapia or cod)
- 1 tsp smoked paprika
- 1 tsp garlic powder
- 1 tsp cumin
- 1 tsp chili powder
- ½ tsp salt
- ½ tsp black pepper
- 10ml olive oil

- 8 corn tortillas
- 100g shredded cabbage
- 1 avocado, sliced
- 1 lime, cut into wedges
- For the Mango Salsa:
- 1 ripe mango, peeled and diced
- 50g diced red onion
- 1 jalapeño pepper, seeded and minced
- 10g chopped fresh coriander
- 1 lime, juiced

Instructions:

1. Preheat the air fryer to 190°C.
2. Rinse the fish fillets and pat dry with a paper towel.
3. In a small bowl, mix together the smoked paprika, garlic powder, cumin, chili powder, salt, and black pepper.
4. Brush the olive oil over both sides of the fish fillets.
5. Sprinkle the spice mixture over the fish, making sure to coat both sides.
6. Place the fish fillets in the air fryer basket or tray.
7. Air fry for 8-10 minutes, or until the fish is cooked through and flakes easily with a fork.
8. In the meantime, prepare the mango salsa by combining the diced mango, red onion, jalapeño pepper, coriander, and lime juice in a mixing bowl. Mix well.
9. Warm the corn tortillas in the air fryer for 1-2 minutes.
10. Assemble the tacos by placing some shredded cabbage on each tortilla, followed by a piece of the cooked fish, sliced avocado, and a spoonful of mango salsa.
11. Serve the fish tacos hot, with lime wedges on the side.

Per serving:

Calories: 373, Carbohydrates: 34g, Fats: 15g, Protein: 28g, Cholesterol: 46mg, fibre: 1g

Air Fryer Lemon Herb Salmon with Roasted Vegetables

Servings: 4

Cooking time: 20 minutes

Ingredients:

- 600g salmon fillets
- 600g mixed vegetables (such as broccoli, peppers, and courgette), chopped
- 2 tablespoons olive oil
- 1 lemon, zested and juiced
- 1 teaspoon dried basil
- 1 teaspoon dried oregano
- Salt and pepper to taste

Instructions:

1. Preheat the air fryer to 180°C.
2. In a bowl, mix together the olive oil, lemon zest, lemon juice, basil, oregano, salt, and pepper.
3. Place the salmon fillets and chopped vegetables in the air fryer basket.
4. Drizzle the olive oil mixture over the salmon and vegetables.
5. Cook in the air fryer for 12-15 minutes, or until the salmon is cooked through and the vegetables are tender.
6. Serve hot and enjoy!

Per serving:

Calories: 320, Carbs: 10g, Fat: 20g, Protein: 28g, Cholesterol: 80mg, Sodium: 150mg, fibre: 4g

Air Fryer Tandoori Chicken Skewers:

Servings: 4

Cooking time: 15 minutes

Ingredients:

- 2 boneless, skinless chicken breasts, cut into 1-inch pieces
- 1 cup plain Greek yogurt

- 2 tablespoons lemon juice
- 1 tablespoon grated ginger
- 2 garlic cloves, minced
- 1 tablespoon garam masala
- 1 teaspoon ground cumin
- 1/2 teaspoon ground turmeric
- Salt and pepper to taste

Instructions:

1. Preheat the air fryer to 190°C.
2. In a small bowl, mix together the Greek yogurt, lemon juice, ginger, garlic, garam masala, cumin, turmeric, salt, and pepper.
3. Thread the chicken pieces onto skewers.
4. Brush the chicken skewers with the yogurt mixture on all sides.
5. Place the skewers in the air fryer basket and cook for 12-15 minutes, or until the chicken is cooked through.
6. Serve the skewers hot with a side of roasted vegetables or salad.

Per serving:

Calories: 190 Carbohydrates: 5g Protein: 31g Fat: 3g Cholesterol: 85mg Sodium: 420mg Fiber: 1g

Garlic Prawns and Broccoli

Servings: 4
Cooking time: 10 minutes

Ingredients:

- 500g prawns, peeled and deveined
- 500g broccoli florets
- 3 tablespoons olive oil
- 1 tablespoon minced garlic
- Salt and pepper to taste

Instructions:

1. Preheat the air fryer to 180°C.
2. In a bowl, mix together the olive oil, minced garlic, salt, and pepper.
3. Add the prawns and broccoli to the bowl and toss until coated.
4. Place the prawns and broccoli in the air fryer basket.
5. Cook in the air fryer for 8-10 minutes, or until the prawns are pink and cooked through and the broccoli is tender.
6. Serve hot and enjoy!

Per serving:

Calories: 210,Carbs: 9g,Fat: 11g,Protein: 21g,Cholesterol: 170mg,Sodium: 350mg,fibre: 3g

Air Fryer Chicken Fajitas

Servings: 4
Cooking time: 20 minutes

Ingredients:

- 500g boneless, skinless chicken breasts, sliced
- 2 peppers, sliced
- 1 onion, sliced
- 2 tablespoons olive oil
- 1 tablespoon chili powder
- 1 tablespoon paprika
- 1 teaspoon garlic powder
- 1 teaspoon onion powder
- Salt and pepper to taste

Instructions:

1. Preheat the air fryer to 180°C.
2. In a bowl, mix together the olive oil, chili powder, paprika, garlic powder, onion powder, salt, and pepper.
3. Add the sliced chicken, peppers, and onion to the bowl and toss until coated.
4. Place the chicken and vegetables in the air fryer basket.
5. Cook in the air fryer for 15-20 minutes, or until the chicken is cooked through and the vegetables are tender.
6. Serve hot and enjoy!

Per serving:

Calories: 260 Carbs: 9g Fat: 11g Protein: 30g Cholesterol: 80mg Sodium: 300mg fibre: 3g

Airfryer Pork Tenderloin with Herbs and Garlic

Servings: 0,

Cooking time: 12 - 15 minutes

Ingredients:

- 200g pork tenderloin
- 1 tablespoon olive oil
- 1 clove garlic, minced
- 1 teaspoon dried thyme
- 1 teaspoon dried rosemary
- Salt and pepper to taste

Instructions:

1. Preheat your airfryer to 180°C for 5 minutes.
2. Rub the pork tenderloin with olive oil, minced garlic, dried thyme, and dried rosemary.
3. Season with salt and pepper to taste.
4. Place the pork tenderloin in the airfryer basket.
5. Cook in the airfryer for 12-15 minutes or until the internal temperature of the pork reaches 63°C.
6. Let the pork rest for 5 minutes before slicing and serving.

Per serving:

Calories: 261 Carbohydrates:2 g Fats: 12.5 g Protein: 35 g Cholesterol: 107 mgSodium: 134 mg Fibre: 0.5 g

Air Fryer Turkey Meatballs with Zucchini Noodles

Serves 2,

Cooking time 10 minutes

Ingredients:

- For the turkey meatballs:
- 454g ground turkey
- 30g breadcrumbs
- 30g grated Parmesan cheese
- 1 egg, lightly beaten
- 1/2 teaspoon garlic powder
- 1/2 teaspoon onion powder
- 1/2 teaspoon dried basil
- 1/2 teaspoon dried oregano
- Salt and pepper, to taste
- For the zucchini noodles:
- 2 medium zucchini
- 1 tablespoon olive oil
- Salt and pepper, to taste

Instructions:

1. Preheat the airfryer to 190°C.
2. In a large mixing bowl, combine the ground turkey, breadcrumbs, Parmesan cheese, egg, garlic powder, onion powder, dried basil, dried oregano, salt, and pepper. Mix well until everything is evenly combined.
3. Use your hands to shape the mixture into 1-inch meatballs.
4. Place the meatballs in the air fryer basket, making sure to leave enough space between each meatball.
5. Air fry the meatballs for 12-15 minutes, or until they are golden brown and cooked through.
6. While the meatballs are cooking, prepare the zucchini noodles. Cut the zucchini into thin, noodle-like strips using a vegetable peeler or spiralizer.
7. Heat the olive oil in a large skillet over medium-high heat. Add the zucchini noodles and cook for 2-3 minutes, or until they are tender and lightly browned.
8. Season the zucchini noodles with salt and pepper to taste.
9. Serve the turkey meatballs with the zucchini noodles on the side. Enjoy!

Per serving (Serves 4):

Calories: 304 Carbs: 7g Fats: 18g Protein:30g Cholesterol: 141mg Sodium: 325mg Fibre: 1g

Chapter 3 Fish and Seafood

Garlic and Herb Prawn Skewers

Serves 2,

Cooking time 10 minutes

Ingredients:
- 250g prawns, peeled and deveined
- 1 tbsp olive oil
- 1 tbsp fresh parsley, chopped
- 1 tbsp fresh basil, chopped
- 2 cloves garlic, minced
- 1/4 tsp salt
- 1/8 tsp black pepper

Instructions:
1. Preheat the airfryer to 180°C.
2. In a bowl, mix together the olive oil, parsley, basil, garlic, salt, and pepper.
3. Thread the prawns onto skewers and brush them with the herb mixture.
4. Place the skewers in the airfryer basket and cook for 8-10 minutes, flipping halfway through.
5. Serve hot.

Per serving:
Calories: 164 Carbs: 1.4g Fats: 7.4g Protein: 23.6g Cholesterol: 172mg Sodium: 383mg Fibre: 0.2g

Crispy Prawn Cakes

Serves 4,

Cooking time 15 minutes

Ingredients:
- 400g prawns, peeled and deveined
- 50 g almond flour
- 2 tbsp coconut flour
- 2 cloves garlic, minced
- 1 tbsp fresh ginger, grated
- 1/4 tsp salt
- 1/4 tsp black pepper
- 1 egg, beaten
- 2 tbsp coconut oil, melted

Instructions:
1. Preheat the airfryer to 200°C.
2. In a food processor, pulse the prawns until finely chopped.
3. In a bowl, mix together the prawns, almond flour, coconut flour, garlic, ginger, salt, and pepper.
4. Add the beaten egg and mix well.
5. Form the mixture into 8 small cakes and brush each cake with melted coconut oil.
6. Place the cakes in the airfryer basket and cook for 12-15 minutes, flipping halfway through.
7. Serve hot with a side of greens.

Per serving:
Calories: 231, Carbs: 4.2g, Fats: 15.8g, Protein: 17.9g, Cholesterol: 200mg, Sodium: 312mg, Fibre: 2.4g

Garlic Butter Prawn Skewers:

Serves: 4

Cooking time: 5-6 minutes

Ingredients:
- 500g prawns, peeled and deveined
- 2 cloves garlic, minced
- 2 tbsp butter, melted
- 1 tbsp olive oil
- 1 tsp lemon juice
- 1/2 tsp salt
- 1/4 tsp black pepper
- Skewers

Instructions:
1. Preheat the air fryer to 180°C.
2. Thread prawns onto skewers.

3. In a small bowl, mix together minced garlic, melted butter, olive oil, lemon juice, salt and black pepper.
4. Brush the garlic butter mixture over the prawns.
5. Place the prawn skewers in the air fryer basket and cook for 5-6 minutes, flipping halfway through, or until cooked through.
6. Serve immediately.

Per serving:

Calories: 156, Carbohydrates: 1g, Fats: 10g, Protein: 14g, Cholesterol: 151mg, Sodium: 381mg, fibre: 0g

Air Fryer Salmon with Lemon and Dill

Serves: 4

Cooking time: 10 minutes

Ingredients:

- 4 salmon fillets
- 1 lemon
- 1 tablespoon chopped fresh dill
- Salt and pepper to taste

Instructions:

1. Preheat the air fryer to 190°C.
2. Season the salmon fillets with salt and pepper on both sides.
3. Cut the lemon into thin slices and place them on the bottom of the air fryer basket.
4. Place the salmon fillets on top of the lemon slices and sprinkle the chopped dill over the fillets.
5. Air fry for 8-10 minutes, or until the salmon is cooked through and flakes easily with a fork.
6. Serve with additional lemon wedges and garnish with extra dill if desired.
7. Air Fryer Chicken and Vegetable Kebabs

Per serving:

Calories: 225 Carbohydrates: 3g Protein: 28g Fat: 11g Cholesterol: 78mg Sodium: 71mg Fiber: 1g

Garlic Parmesan Crusted Salmon

Servings: 2

Cooking time: 12 minutes

Ingredients:

- 280g salmon fillet
- 1 tbsp olive oil
- 1/2 tsp garlic powder
- 1/2 tsp onion powder
- 1/4 tsp paprika
- 1/4 tsp salt
- 1/4 tsp black pepper
- 15g grated Parmesan cheese

Instructions:

1. Preheat the air fryer to 200°C.
2. Brush the salmon fillets with olive oil and season with salt and pepper.
3. Place the salmon in the air fryer basket and cook for 10-12 minutes, depending on the thickness of the fillets.
4. Check the internal temperature of the salmon with a meat thermometer. It should read 63°C.
5. Serve hot.

Per serving:

Calories: 354, Carbohydrates:2g, Protein: 32g, Fat: 25g, Cholesterol: 94mg, Sodium: 526mg, fibre: 0.3g

Cajun Tilapia

Serves 4

Cooking time: 15 minutes

Ingredients:

- 500g tilapia fillets
- 2 tsp paprika
- 1 tsp onion powder
- 1 tsp garlic powder

- 1 tsp dried thyme
- 1 tsp dried oregano
- 1/2 tsp cayenne pepper
- 1/2 tsp salt
- 1/4 tsp black pepper
- 2 tbsp olive oil

Instructions:

1. Preheat the air fryer to 200°C.
2. In a small bowl, mix together the paprika, onion powder, garlic powder, thyme, oregano, cayenne pepper, salt, and black pepper.
3. Rub the spice mixture onto both sides of the tilapia fillets.
4. Drizzle the olive oil over the tilapia fillets.
5. Place the tilapia fillets in the air fryer basket and cook for 10-12 minutes or until the fish is cooked through and flakes easily with a fork.
6. Serve with a side of steamed vegetables.

Per serving:

Calories: 177kcal, Carbohydrates: 2g, Protein: 25g, Fat: 7g, Cholesterol: 58mg, Sodium: 361mg fibre: 1g

Grilled Lemon Herb Halibut

Serves 4,

Cooking time 12-15 minutes

Ingredients:

- 600g halibut fillets
- 2 tablespoons olive oil
- 2 cloves garlic, minced
- 1 tablespoon fresh lemon juice
- 1 teaspoon dried basil
- 1 teaspoon dried oregano
- Salt and black pepper, to taste

Instructions:

1. Preheat the airfryer to 200°C.
2. Season the halibut fillets with salt and black pepper.
3. In a small bowl, mix together the olive oil, garlic, lemon juice, dried basil, and dried oregano.
4. Brush the halibut fillets with the herb mixture.
5. Place the halibut fillets in the airfryer basket and cook for 12-15 minutes, or until the fish is cooked through and flakes easily with a fork.
6. Serve hot with your choice of sides.

Per serving:

Calories: 234, Carbs: 2g, Fat: 14g, Protein: 25g, Cholesterol: 54mg, Sodium: 214mg, Fibre: 0g

Lemon Garlic Baked Cod

Serves 4

Cooking time 10-12 minutes

Ingredients:

- 600g cod fillets
- 2 tablespoons olive oil
- 2 cloves garlic, minced
- 1 tablespoon fresh lemon juice
- 1 teaspoon lemon zest
- Salt and black pepper, to taste

Instructions:

1. Preheat the airfryer to 180°C.
2. Season the cod fillets with salt and black pepper.
3. In a small bowl, mix together the olive oil, garlic, lemon juice, and lemon zest.
4. Brush the cod fillets with the lemon mixture.
5. Place the cod fillets in the airfryer basket and cook for 10-12 minutes, or until the fish is cooked through and flakes easily with a fork.
6. Serve hot with your choice of sides.

Per serving:

Calories: 225, Carbs: 1g, Fat: 9g, Protein: 34g, Cholesterol: 70mg, Sodium: 200mg, Fibre: 0g

Crispy salmon with lemon and dill

Servings: 4

Cooking time: 10 minutes

Ingredients:
- 4 salmon fillets, skin on (120g each)
- 1 tablespoon olive oil
- 1/2 teaspoon salt
- 1/4 teaspoon black pepper
- 1 lemon, sliced
- 1 tablespoon fresh dill, chopped

Instructions:
1. Preheat the air fryer to 200°C.
2. Pat the salmon fillets dry with a paper towel and place them skin-side down in the air fryer basket.
3. Drizzle the olive oil over the salmon and season with salt and pepper.
4. Place a few slices of lemon on top of each fillet.
5. Air fry the salmon for 8-10 minutes, or until the internal temperature reaches 63°C.
6. Sprinkle fresh dill on top of the salmon and serve immediately.

Per serving:
Calories: 226, kcal Fat: 11g Saturated Fat: 2g, Cholesterol: 83mg, Sodium: 356mg, Carbohydrates: 3g, fibre: 1g, Sugar: 1g, Protein: 27g

Air Fryer Mackerel Fillets

Serves: 2

Cooking time: 12 minutes

Ingredients:
- 2 mackerel fillets
- 1 tablespoon olive oil
- 1/4 teaspoon sea salt
- 1/4 teaspoon black pepper
- 1/2 teaspoon smoked paprika
- 1/2 teaspoon garlic powder

Instructions:
1. Preheat the air fryer to 200°C.
2. Pat the mackerel fillets dry with paper towels and brush them with olive oil.
3. In a small bowl, mix together the sea salt, black pepper, smoked paprika, and garlic powder.
4. Rub the spice mixture all over the mackerel fillets.
5. Place the fillets in the air fryer basket and cook for 10-12 minutes, or until they are cooked through and golden brown.
6. Serve with your favourite side dishes.

Per serving:
Calories: 263, Carbohydrates: 0g, Protein: 23g, Fat: 19g, Saturated Fat: 3g, Cholesterol: 70mg, Sodium: 329mg, fibre: 0g, Sugar: 0g

Air Fryer Trout with Lemon and Thyme

Serves: 2

Cooking time: 10 minutes

Ingredients:
- 2 trout fillets
- 2 tablespoons olive oil
- 1 tablespoon fresh thyme leaves
- 1 lemon, thinly sliced
- Sea salt and black pepper, to taste

Instructions:
1. Preheat the air fryer to 200°C.
2. Rub the trout fillets with olive oil and season them with sea salt and black pepper.
3. Arrange the lemon slices and thyme leaves on top of the fillets.
4. Place the fillets in the air fryer basket and cook for 8-10 minutes, or until they are cooked through and the skin is crispy.

5. Serve with your favourite side dishes.

Per serving:

Calories: 259, Carbohydrates: 2g, Protein: 22g, Fat: 18g, Saturated Fat: 3g, Cholesterol: 60mg, Sodium: 70mg, fibre: 1g, Sugar: 1g

Air Fryer Tuna Steaks with Sesame Seeds

Serves: 2

Cooking time: 8 minutes

Ingredients:

- 2 tuna steaks
- 1 tablespoon olive oil
- 1 tablespoon sesame seeds
- 1/2 teaspoon sea salt
- 1/4 teaspoon black pepper

Instructions:

1. Preheat the air fryer to 200°C.
2. Brush the tuna steaks with olive oil.
3. Mix together the sesame seeds, sea salt, and black pepper in a small bowl.
4. Rub the spice mixture all over the tuna steaks.
5. Place the steaks in the air fryer basket and cook for 6-8 minutes, or until they are cooked through but still slightly pink in the center.
6. Serve with your favourite side dishes.

Per serving:

Calories: 235, Carbohydrates: 1g, Protein: 33g, Fat: 10g, Saturated Fat: 2g, Cholesterol: 58mg, Sodium: 609mg, fibre: 1g, Sugar: 0g

Air Fryer Blackened Salmon

Serves: 2

Cooking time: 10 minutes

Ingredients:

- 2 salmon fillets (about 200g each)
- 1 tbsp paprika
- 1 tsp dried thyme
- 1 tsp garlic powder
- 1/2 tsp cayenne pepper
- 1/4 tsp salt
- 1/4 tsp black pepper
- 1 tbsp olive oil

Instructions:

1. Preheat the air fryer to 200°C.
2. Mix the paprika, dried thyme, garlic powder, cayenne pepper, salt, and black pepper in a small bowl.
3. Brush the salmon fillets with olive oil on both sides.
4. Rub the seasoning mix all over the salmon fillets.
5. Place the salmon fillets in the air fryer basket and cook for 8-10 minutes or until cooked through.

Per serving:

Calories: 338 kcal, Fat: 21g, Carbohydrates: 2g, Protein: 35g

Air Fryer Tuna Steaks with Lemon and Herbs

Serves: 2

Cooking time: 8 minutes

Ingredients:

- 2 tuna steaks (about 150g each)
- 1 tbsp olive oil
- 1 tsp dried thyme
- 1 tsp dried oregano
- 1/4 tsp salt
- 1/4 tsp black pepper
- 1 lemon, sliced

Instructions:

1. Preheat the air fryer to 200°C.
2. Brush the tuna steaks with olive oil on both sides.
3. Mix the dried thyme, dried oregano, salt, and black pepper in a small bowl.

4. Rub the seasoning mix all over the tuna steaks.
5. Place the tuna steaks and lemon slices in the air fryer basket and cook for 8 minutes or until cooked through.

Per serving:

Calories: 249 kcal, Fat: 9g, Carbohydrates: 4g, Protein: 37g

Air Fryer Coconut Prawns

Serves: 4

Cooking time: 10 minutes

Ingredients:

- 500g large prawns, peeled and deveined
- 60 g shredded coconut
- 55 g panko breadcrumbs
- 1 tsp garlic powder
- 1/2 tsp paprika
- 1/4 tsp salt
- 1/4 tsp black pepper
- 2 eggs, beaten

Instructions:

1. Preheat the air fryer to 200°C.
2. In a small bowl, mix the shredded coconut, panko breadcrumbs, garlic powder, paprika, salt, and black pepper.
3. Dip the prawns in the beaten eggs, then coat them in the coconut mixture.
4. Place the coated prawns in the air fryer basket and spray with cooking spray.
5. Cook for 5 minutes, then flip the prawns and cook for another 5 minutes or until golden brown.

Per serving:

Calories: 239 kcal, Fat: 8g, Carbohydrates: 12g, Protein: 30g

Air Fryer Battered Fish

Serves: 4

Cooking time: 10 minutes

Ingredients:

- 4 fillets of white fish, such as cod or haddock (120g each)
- 50g almond flour
- 50g coconut flour
- 1 tsp paprika
- 1 tsp garlic powder
- 1/2 tsp salt
- 1/4 tsp black pepper
- 1 large egg
- 120ml unsweetened almond milk
- Cooking spray

Instructions:

1. Preheat the air fryer to 200°C.
2. In a bowl, whisk together the almond flour, coconut flour, paprika, garlic powder, salt, and black pepper.
3. In another bowl, beat the egg and whisk in the almond milk.
4. Dip each fillet into the egg mixture, then coat with the flour mixture.
5. Place the fillets in the air fryer basket, spray with cooking spray, and cook for 10 minutes or until the fish is cooked through and the coating is crispy.

Per serving:

Calories: 227, Fat: 11g, Carbohydrates: 6g, fibre: 3g, Protein: 24g, Sugar: 1g, Sodium: 442mg

Oat-Coated Fish

Serves: 2

Cooking time: 12-15 minutes

Ingredients

- 300g white fish fillets, such as cod or haddock
- 50g oats

- 1/2 tsp paprika
- 1/2 tsp garlic powder
- 1/4 tsp salt
- 1/4 tsp black pepper
- 1 egg, beaten

Instructions:

1. Preheat the air fryer to 200°C.
2. Cut the fish fillets into strips.
3. In a shallow dish, mix together the oats, paprika, garlic powder, salt, and black pepper.
4. Dip each fish strip into the beaten egg, then coat with the oat mixture.
5. Place the fish strips in a single layer in the air fryer basket.
6. Cook in the air fryer for 12-15 minutes, or until the fish is cooked through and the coating is crispy and golden brown.
7. Serve with a side of vegetables or a salad.

Per serving:

Calories: 234 kcal, Total Fat: 6.8 g, Saturated Fat: 1.5 g, Cholesterol: 130 mg, Sodium: 399 mg, Total Carbohydrate: 11.7 g, Dietary fibre: 2.3 g, Total Sugars: 0.6 g, Protein: 33.5 g

Air Fryer Fish Tempura

Serves 4,

Cooking time 15 minutes

Ingredients:

- 4 white fish fillets, such as tilapia or cod
- 50 g oat flour
- 60 g cornflour
- 1/2 tsp. baking powder
- 1/2 tsp. salt
- 1/4 tsp. black pepper
- 120 ml cold water
- 1 large egg
- 1 tbsp. vegetable oil
- Cooking spray

Instructions:

1. Preheat the air fryer to 200°C
2. In a mixing bowl, whisk together oat flour, cornflour, baking powder, salt, and black pepper.
3. In a separate mixing bowl, beat together the egg, cold water, and vegetable oil.
4. Dip each fish fillet into the wet mixture, then into the dry mixture, pressing down to coat well.
5. Place the coated fish fillets in a single layer in the air fryer basket.
6. Lightly coat the fish fillets with cooking spray.
7. Air fry the fish for 10-12 minutes or until the fish is golden brown and cooked through.
8. Serve the fish hot with your choice of dipping sauce.

Per serving:

Calories 228, Fat: 7g, Protein:23g, Carbohydrates: 20g Sodium:458mg Fibre: 1g

Air Fryer Lemon Garlic Salmon

Serves: 2

Cooking time: 12 minutes

Ingredients:

- 2 salmon fillets
- 1 tablespoon olive oil
- 1 tablespoon lemon juice
- 2 cloves garlic, minced
- Salt and pepper, to taste

Instructions:

1. Preheat the air fryer to 200°C.
2. Pat dry the salmon fillets with paper towels.
3. In a small bowl, mix together olive oil, lemon juice, minced garlic, salt, and pepper.
4. Brush the mixture onto both sides of the salmon fillets.
5. Place the salmon fillets into the air fryer basket and cook for 12 minutes or until the

internal temperature reaches 63°C.

Per serving:

Calories 260, Fat: 14g, Protein:30g, Carbohydrates: 1g Sodium:80mg Fibre: 1g

Air Fryer Tuna Fish Cakes

Serves: 4

Cooking time: 12 minutes

Ingredients:

- 2 cans (125 g each) tuna, drained
- 50 g almond flour
- 40 g chopped onion
- 35 g chopped celery
- 40 g chopped red pepper
- 1 egg
- 1 tablespoon Dijon mustard
- 1 tablespoon lemon juice
- 1 teaspoon dried dill
- Salt and pepper, to taste
- Cooking spray

Instructions:

1. In a medium bowl, mix together tuna, almond flour, chopped onion, chopped celery, chopped red pepper, egg, Dijon mustard, lemon juice, dried dill, salt, and pepper.
2. Form the mixture into 8 fish cakes..
3. Preheat the air fryer to 190°C.
4. Spray the air fryer basket with cooking spray.
5. Place the tuna fish cakes into the air fryer basket and cook for 12 minutes, flipping halfway through.

Per serving:

Calories 208, Fat: 8g, Protein:30g, Carbohydrates: 4g Sodium:326mg Fibre: 2g

Spicy Prawns:

Serves 2

Cooking time: 10 minutes

Ingredients:

- 200g prawns, peeled and deveined
- 1 tablespoon olive oil
- 1 teaspoon paprika
- 1/2 teaspoon garlic powder
- 1/2 teaspoon onion powder
- 1/4 teaspoon cayenne pepper
- Salt and pepper to taste
- Lemon wedges for serving

Instructions:

1. In a large bowl, combine the prawns, olive oil, paprika, garlic powder, onion powder, cayenne pepper, salt, and pepper. Toss to coat the prawns evenly.
2. Preheat the air fryer to 200°C.
3. Once the air fryer is preheated, place the prawns in a single layer in the air fryer basket.
4. Air fry the prawns for 8-10 minutes, or until they are cooked through and crispy.
5. Serve the shrimp immediately with lemon wedges on the side.

Per serving:

Calories168, Fat: 7g, Protein:21g, Carbohydrates: 4g Sodium:575mg Fibre: 1g

Chapter 4 Poultry

Chicken Tenders

Serves: 4

Cooking time:

- 500g chicken breast mini fillets
- 50g almond flour
- 50g grated parmesan cheese
- 1 tsp garlic powder
- 1 tsp onion powder
- 1 tsp smoked paprika
- 1/2 tsp salt
- 1/4 tsp black pepper
- 2 large eggs, beaten

Instructions:

1. Preheat air fryer to 200°C.
2. In a shallow dish, mix together almond flour, parmesan cheese, garlic powder, onion powder, smoked paprika, salt, and black pepper.
3. In another shallow dish, beat the eggs.
4. Dip each chicken mini fillet in the egg mixture, then coat with the almond flour mixture, pressing the coating onto the chicken to make sure it sticks.
5. Place the chicken tenders in a single layer in the air fryer basket. You may need to work in batches depending on the size of your air fryer.
6. Air fry the chicken tenders for 10-12 minutes, flipping them over halfway through, until they are golden brown and cooked through.
7. Serve hot with your favourite dipping sauce.

Per serving:

Calories 250, Fat: 11g, Protein:35g, Carbohydrates: 2g Sodium:490mg Fibre: 1g

Air Fryer Turkey Breast

Serves: 4

Cooking time: 45 minutes

Ingredients:

- 600g boneless turkey breast
- 2 tbsp olive oil
- 2 tsp dried oregano
- 2 tsp garlic powder
- 1 tsp smoked paprika
- Salt and pepper to taste

Instructions:

1. Preheat the air fryer to 180°C.
2. In a small bowl, mix together the olive oil, oregano, garlic powder, smoked paprika, salt and pepper.
3. Brush the turkey breast with the oil and spice mixture.
4. Place the turkey breast in the air fryer basket and cook for 40-45 minutes, or until the internal temperature reaches 75°C.
5. Let the turkey breast rest for 5 minutes before slicing and serving.

Per serving:

Calories:267, Fat: 10g, Protein:41g, Carbohydrates: 2g Sodium:87mg Fibre: 0g

Air Fryer Duck Breast with Orange Glaze

Serves: 2

Cooking time: 30 minutes

Ingredients:

- 2 duck breasts
- 2 tbsp honey
- Juice and zest of 1 orange

- 1 tbsp soy sauce
- 1 tsp garlic powder
- Salt and pepper to taste

Instructions:

1. Preheat the air fryer to 200°C.
2. Score the skin of the duck breasts in a criss-cross pattern.
3. In a small bowl, whisk together the honey, orange juice and zest, soy sauce, garlic powder, salt and pepper.
4. Brush the glaze onto the duck breasts, making sure to coat the skin side well.
5. Place the duck breasts skin-side down in the air fryer basket and cook for 15 minutes.
6. Flip the duck breasts and brush the skin with more glaze.
7. Cook for another 10-15 minutes, or until the internal temperature reaches 70°C.
8. Let the duck breasts rest for 5 minutes before slicing and serving.

Per serving:

Calories: 394, Fat: 23g, Protein:25g, Carbohydrates: 23g Sodium:605mg Fibre: 0g

Air Fryer Lemon and Herb Chicken Thighs

Serves: 4

Cooking time: 30 minutes

Ingredients:

- 4 chicken thighs, bone-in and skin-on
- Juice and zest of 1 lemon
- 2 cloves garlic, minced
- 2 tbsp olive oil
- 1 tsp dried thyme
- 1 tsp dried rosemary
- Salt and pepper to taste

Instructions:

1. Preheat the air fryer to 190°C.
2. In a small bowl, whisk together the lemon juice and zest, garlic, olive oil, thyme, rosemary, salt and pepper.
3. Brush the mixture onto the chicken thighs, making sure to coat all sides.
4. Place the chicken thighs in the air fryer basket, skin-side up.
5. Cook for 25-30 minutes, or until the internal temperature reaches 75°C.
6. Let the chicken thighs rest for 5 minutes before serving.

Per serving:

Calories: 317, Fat: 23g, Protein:24g, Carbohydrates: 2g Sodium:178mg Fibre: 1g

Air Fryer Lemon Garlic Turkey Breast

Serves: 4

Cooking time: 40 minutes

Ingredients:

- 600g turkey breast
- 1 lemon, juiced
- 2 garlic cloves, minced
- 1 tsp dried thyme
- 1 tsp dried rosemary
- 1 tsp dried oregano
- 1/2 tsp salt
- 1/4 tsp black pepper
- 2 tbsp olive oil

Instructions:

1. Preheat the air fryer to 180°C.
2. In a small bowl, mix together the lemon juice, garlic, thyme, rosemary, oregano, salt, pepper, and olive oil.
3. Place the turkey breast in a shallow dish and pour the marinade over it, making sure to coat the turkey breast evenly.
4. Place the turkey breast in the air fryer basket

and cook for 35-40 minutes, or until the internal temperature reaches 75°C.
5. Let the turkey breast rest for 5-10 minutes before slicing and serving.

Per serving:

Calories: 270, Fat: 10g, Protein:41g, Carbohydrates: 2g Sodium:343mg Fibre: 1g

Air Fryer BBQ Chicken Wings

Serves: 4

Cooking time: 25 minutes

Ingredients:

- 800g chicken wings
- 1/2 tsp salt
- 1/2 tsp black pepper
- 1/2 tsp garlic powder
- 1/2 tsp onion powder
- 1/2 tsp paprika
- 1/2 tsp cumin
- 60 g low-sugar BBQ sauce

Instructions:

1. Preheat the air fryer to 200°C.
2. In a small bowl, mix together the salt, black pepper, garlic powder, onion powder, paprika, and cumin.
3. Place the chicken wings in a large bowl and sprinkle the spice mixture over them, making sure to coat them evenly.
4. Place the chicken wings in the air fryer basket and cook for 20-25 minutes, flipping them halfway through the Cooking time.
5. Brush the BBQ sauce over the chicken wings and cook for an additional 2-3 minutes.
6. Serve immediately.

Per serving:

Calories: 285, Fat: 19g, Protein:24g, Carbohydrates: 4g Sodium:465mg Fibre: 0g

Air Fryer Chicken Satay

Serves: 4

Cooking time: 20 minutes

Ingredients:

- 4 boneless, skinless chicken breasts (400g), cut into bite-sized pieces
- 1 tablespoon olive oil
- 1 tablespoon soy sauce
- 2 cloves garlic, minced
- 1 teaspoon ground coriander
- 1 teaspoon ground cumin
- 1/2 teaspoon turmeric
- 1/2 teaspoon ground ginger
- 1/2 teaspoon salt
- 1/4 teaspoon black pepper
- 8 bamboo skewers, soaked in water for 30 minutes

Instructions:

1. Preheat the air fryer to 190°C.
2. In a large bowl, whisk together the olive oil, soy sauce, garlic, coriander, cumin, turmeric, ginger, salt, and black pepper.
3. Add the chicken to the bowl and toss to coat.
4. Thread the chicken onto the skewers.
5. Place the skewers in the air fryer basket and cook for 10 minutes.
6. Flip the skewers over and cook for an additional 10 minutes, or until the chicken is cooked through and lightly browned.
7. Serve hot with peanut sauce or your favourite dipping sauce.

Per serving:

Calories: 187, Fat: 5g, Protein:32g, Carbohydrates: 2g Sodium:618mg Fibre: 0.5g

Air Fryer Chicken Satay Skewers

Servings: 4

Cooking time: 10 minutes

Ingredients:
- 500g boneless, skinless chicken breasts, cut into cubes
- 1/4 cup natural peanut butter
- 2 tablespoons coconut aminos (or soy sauce)
- 2 tablespoons lime juice
- 2 tablespoons honey
- 1 garlic clove, minced
- Salt and pepper to taste
- Skewers

Instructions:
1. Preheat the air fryer to 190°C.
2. In a large bowl, combine the chicken cubes, peanut butter, coconut aminos, lime juice, honey, garlic, salt, and pepper. Mix well to coat.
3. Thread the chicken onto skewers.
4. Place the skewers in the air fryer basket and cook for 10 minutes, flipping them halfway through, until the chicken is cooked through and the skewers are lightly charred.
5. Serve hot, with extra sauce if desired.

Per serving:
Calories: 280 Carbohydrates: 21g Protein: 30g Fat: 8g Cholesterol: 120mg Sodium: 620mg Fibre: 1g

Air Fryer Turkey Burgers

Servings: 4

Cooking time: 15 minutes

Ingredients:
- 500g turkey mince
- 50 g oat flour
- 25 g grated Parmesan cheese
- 1 egg
- 1/2 teaspoon salt
- 1/4 teaspoon black pepper
- 1/2 teaspoon garlic powder
- 1/2 teaspoon onion powder
- 1/2 teaspoon dried oregano
- 1/2 teaspoon dried basil

Instructions:
1. Preheat air fryer to 190°C.
2. In a mixing bowl, combine turkey mince, oat flour, Parmesan cheese, egg, salt, black pepper, garlic powder, onion powder, dried oregano, and dried basil. Mix until well combined.
3. Divide the mixture into 4 portions and shape into patties.
4. Place the patties in the air fryer basket and cook for 15 minutes or until fully cooked, flipping halfway through.
5. Serve on a bun with your favourite toppings.

Per serving:
Calories: 272, Fat: 11g, Protein:37g, Carbohydrates: 7g Sodium:518mg Fibre: 1g

Air Fryer Turkey Meatballs

Serves: 4

Cooking time: 25 minutes

Ingredients:
- 500g turkey mince
- 40 g rolled oats
- 25 g grated Parmesan cheese
- 1 egg
- 1 tbsp dried parsley
- 1 tsp garlic powder
- 1 tsp onion powder
- Salt and pepper, to taste
- Cooking spray

Instructions:
1. In a large bowl, mix together the turkey mince, rolled oats, Parmesan cheese, egg, parsley, garlic powder, onion powder, salt, and pepper until everything is well combined.
2. Preheat the air fryer to 200°C.
3. Using your hands, shape the turkey mixture into 12 meatballs.
4. Spray the air fryer basket with cooking spray and place the meatballs in the basket.
5. Cook the meatballs in the air fryer for 20-25 minutes or until they are cooked through and golden brown.
6. Serve hot with your favourite sauce or dipping sauce.

Per serving:
Calories: 201, Fat: 9g, Protein:24g, Carbohydrates: 5g Sodium:165mg Fibre: 1g

Air Fryer Lemon Pepper Chicken

Servings: 4

Ingredients:
- 4 boneless, skinless chicken breasts
- 1 tablespoon olive oil
- 1 teaspoon salt
- 1 teaspoon black pepper
- 2 teaspoons garlic powder
- 2 teaspoons onion powder
- 2 teaspoons dried parsley
- 1 lemon, juiced and zested

Instructions:
1. Preheat air fryer to 195°C.
2. In a small bowl, mix together olive oil, salt, black pepper, garlic powder, onion powder, dried parsley, lemon juice, and lemon zest.
3. Pat the chicken breasts dry with paper towels, then rub the olive oil mixture all over the chicken.
4. Place the chicken breasts in the air fryer basket, making sure they are not touching.
5. Cook for 10 minutes, then flip the chicken over and cook for another 8-10 minutes or until the internal temperature of the chicken reaches 74°C.
6. Serve immediately with a side of your choice.

Per serving:
Calories: 215, Fat: 7g, Protein:35g, Carbohydrates: 2g Sodium:638mg Fibre: 0g

Honey Mustard Turkey Breast:

Serves 4 Cooking time: 30 minutes

Ingredients:
- 4 turkey breast fillets (600g)
- 1 tablespoon olive oil
- 2 tablespoons honey mustard
- 1 tablespoon honey
- 1/2 teaspoon garlic powder
- Salt and pepper to taste

Instructions:
1. Preheat the air fryer to 180°C.
2. Brush the turkey fillets with olive oil and season with salt and pepper.
3. In a small bowl, whisk together the honey mustard, honey, and garlic powder.
4. Coat the turkey fillets with the honey mustard mixture.
5. Place the turkey fillets in the air fryer basket and cook for 15 minutes.
6. Flip the turkey fillets and cook for another 10-12 minutes or until the internal temperature reaches 74°C.
7. Serve hot.

Per serving:
Calories: 207, Fat: 5g, Protein:33g, Carbohydrates: 7g Sodium:233mg Fibre: 0g

Crispy Duck Legs:

Serves 2 Cooking time: 40 minutes

Ingredients:
- 2 duck legs (400g)
- 1 tablespoon five spice powder
- 1 teaspoon salt
- 1/2 teaspoon garlic powder
- 1/4 teaspoon black pepper
- 30 g cornflour

Instructions:
1. Preheat the air fryer to 180°C.
2. In a small bowl, mix together the five spice powder, salt, garlic powder, black pepper, and cornstarch.
3. Pat the duck legs dry with paper towels and rub the spice mixture all over them.
4. Place the duck legs in the air fryer basket and cook for 20 minutes.
5. Flip the duck legs and cook for another 15-20 minutes or until the internal temperature reaches 74°C and the skin is crispy.
6. Serve hot.

Per serving:
Calories: 444, Fat: 29g, Protein:32g, Carbohydrates: 16g Sodium:1315mg Fibre: 0g

Airfryer Cajun Chicken Thighs

Serves: 4

Cooking time: 25 minutes

Ingredients:
- 8 bone-in, skin-on chicken thighs
- 1 tablespoon paprika
- 1 tablespoon garlic powder
- 1 tablespoon onion powder
- 1 tablespoon dried oregano
- 1 tablespoon dried thyme
- 1 teaspoon cayenne pepper
- 1 teaspoon black pepper
- 1 teaspoon salt

Instructions:
1. Preheat the airfryer to 200°C.
2. In a small bowl, mix together the paprika, garlic powder, onion powder, oregano, thyme, cayenne pepper, black pepper, and salt.
3. Rub the seasoning mixture all over the chicken thighs.
4. Place the chicken thighs in the airfryer

basket, skin-side up.

5. Airfry for 25 minutes, or until the internal temperature of the chicken reaches 75°C.

Per serving:
Calories: 310, Fat: 19g, Protein:32g, Carbohydrates: 3g Sodium:580mg Fibre: 1g

Airfryer Teriyaki Turkey Meatballs

Serves: 4

Cooking time: 15 minutes

Ingredients:
- 455 g turkey mince
- 25 g almond flour
- 30 g chopped onions
- 1 tablespoon minced garlic
- 1 tablespoon grated ginger
- 2 tablespoons low-sodium soy sauce
- 1 tablespoon rice vinegar
- 1 tablespoon honey
- 1/4 teaspoon black pepper

Instructions:
1. Preheat the airfryer to 190°C.
2. In a large bowl, combine the turkey mince, almond flour, onions, garlic, ginger, and black pepper. Mix well.
3. Form the mixture into 16 meatballs.
4. Place the meatballs in the airfryer basket.
5. In a small bowl, whisk together the soy sauce, rice vinegar, and honey.
6. Pour the teriyaki sauce over the meatballs.
7. Airfry for 15 minutes, or until the meatballs are cooked through.

Per serving:
Calories: 220, Fat: 11g, Protein:23g, Carbohydrates: 7g Sodium:618mg Fibre: 1g

Chicken Kiev

Servings: 2

Cooking time: 30 minutes

Ingredients:
- 2 boneless, skinless chicken breasts
- 50g unsalted butter, at room temperature
- 1 garlic clove, minced
- 1 tablespoon chopped fresh parsley
- 1 tablespoon chopped fresh chives
- 1/2 teaspoon salt
- 1/4 teaspoon black pepper
- 40g plain flour
- 1 egg, beaten
- 60g panko breadcrumbs
- Cooking spray

Instructions:
1. Preheat the air fryer to 180°C.
2. In a small bowl, mix together the butter, garlic, parsley, chives, salt, and pepper until well combined.
3. Cut a slit lengthwise in each chicken breast, creating a pocket. Stuff each pocket with half of the butter mixture and seal with toothpicks.
4. Place the flour, beaten egg, and panko breadcrumbs into separate bowls.
5. Roll each chicken breast in the flour, then the egg, and finally the breadcrumbs, making sure to coat them well.
6. Lightly spray the chicken breasts with cooking spray.
7. Place the chicken breasts in the air fryer basket and cook for 25 minutes, flipping them over halfway through the Cooking time.
8. Remove the toothpicks before serving.

Per serving:
Calories: 455, Fat: 19g, Protein: 42g, Carbohydrates: 0g Sodium:778mg Fibre: 1g

Air Fryer Teriyaki Chicken Thighs

Serves: 4

Cooking time: 20 minutes

Ingredients:
- 4 bone-in, skin-on chicken thighs
- 60 ml low-sodium soy sauce
- 60 g honey
- 1 tbsp rice vinegar
- 1 tbsp minced garlic
- 1 tbsp minced ginger
- 1/4 tsp black pepper
- 2 tsp cornflour
- 2 tsp cold water
- 30 g chopped spring onions
- Sesame seeds, for garnish

Instructions:
1. Preheat the air fryer to 200°C.
2. In a small bowl, whisk together the soy sauce, honey, rice vinegar, minced garlic, minced ginger, and black pepper.
3. Place the chicken thighs in the air fryer basket and brush with the teriyaki sauce.
4. Air fry for 15-18 minutes, until the internal temperature reaches 65°C, flipping the chicken halfway through.
5. While the chicken is cooking, mix the cornflour and cold water in a small bowl to create a slurry.
6. In a small saucepan, bring the remaining teriyaki sauce to a boil over medium-high heat.
7. Whisk in the cornflour slurry and stir for 1-2 minutes until the sauce thickens.
8. Brush the thickened sauce over the cooked chicken thighs and garnish with chopped spring onions and sesame seeds.

Per serving:
Calories: 306, Fat: 11g, Protein: 31g, Carbohydrates: 0g Sodium:550mg Fibre: 0g

Air Fryer Garlic Rosemary Turkey Breast

Serves: 6

Cooking time: 35 minutes

Ingredients:
- 1 boneless turkey breast (about 900 g)
- 2 tbsp olive oil
- 2 tsp minced garlic
- 2 tsp chopped fresh rosemary
- 1 tsp salt
- 1/4 tsp black pepper

Instructions:
1. Preheat the air fryer to 180°C.
2. In a small bowl, mix together the olive oil, minced garlic, chopped rosemary, kosher salt, and black pepper.
3. Pat the turkey breast dry with paper towels and place it in the air fryer basket.
4. Brush the garlic rosemary mixture all over the turkey breast.
5. Air fry for 30-35 minutes, until the internal temperature reaches 70°C.
6. Let the turkey breast rest for 5-10 minutes before slicing and serving.

Per serving:
Calories: 212, Fat: 9g, Protein: 30g, Carbohydrates: 0g Sodium:427mg Fibre: 0g

Chapter 5 Pork, Beef and Lamb

Air Fryer Pork Chops

Serves 2

Cooking time: 15 minutes

Ingredients:

- 2 boneless pork chops
- 1/2 tsp smoked paprika
- 1/2 tsp garlic powder
- 1/2 tsp onion powder
- Salt and pepper, to taste

Instructions:

1. Preheat the air fryer to 200°C.
2. In a small bowl, mix together the smoked paprika, garlic powder, onion powder, salt, and pepper.
3. Season the pork chops with the spice mixture, making sure to coat both sides evenly.
4. Place the pork chops in the air fryer basket and cook for 10-15 minutes, flipping halfway through, until the internal temperature reaches 63°C.

Per serving:

Calories: 230, Fat: 10g, Protein: 30g, Carbohydrates: 1g Sodium:375mg Fibre: 0g

Air Fryer Pork Tenderloin

Serves 4

Cooking time: 20 minutes

Ingredients:

- 455 g pork tenderloin
- 2 tbsp olive oil
- 1/2 tsp dried thyme
- 1/2 tsp dried rosemary
- 1/2 tsp garlic powder
- Salt and pepper, to taste

Instructions:

1. Preheat the air fryer to 200°C.
2. Rub the pork tenderloin with olive oil.
3. Mix together the dried thyme, dried rosemary, garlic powder, salt, and pepper in a small bowl.
4. Rub the spice mixture over the pork tenderloin, making sure to coat all sides evenly.
5. Place the pork tenderloin in the air fryer basket and cook for 20 minutes, flipping halfway through, until the internal temperature reaches 63°C.

Per serving:

Calories: 240, Fat: 11g, Protein: 30g, Carbohydrates: 1g Sodium:516mg Fibre: 0g

Air Fryer Pork Belly Bites

Serves 4

Cooking time: 20 minutes

Ingredients:

- 455 g pork belly, cut into bite-sized pieces
- 1 tbsp olive oil
- 1/2 tsp smoked paprika
- 1/2 tsp garlic powder
- 1/2 tsp onion powder
- Salt and pepper, to taste

Instructions:

1. Preheat the air fryer to 200°C.
2. In a small bowl, mix together the smoked paprika, garlic powder, onion powder, salt, and pepper.
3. Toss the pork belly pieces with olive oil and the spice mixture, making sure to coat all pieces evenly.
4. Place the pork belly pieces in the air fryer

basket and cook for 15-20 minutes, shaking the basket halfway through, until crispy and cooked through.

Per serving:

Calories: 310, Fat: 29g, Protein: 9g, Carbohydrates: 9g Sodium:905mg Fibre: 0g

Air Fryer Pork Chops with Mustard Crust

Serves: 4

Cooking time: 12 minutes

Ingredients:

- 4 bone-in pork chops
- 2 tablespoons Dijon mustard
- 2 tablespoons olive oil
- 1 tablespoon honey
- 1 teaspoon smoked paprika
- 1/2 teaspoon garlic powder
- 1/4 teaspoon salt
- 1/4 teaspoon black pepper
- 50 g breadcrumbs

Instructions:

1. Preheat the air fryer to 200°C.
2. Season the pork chops with salt and pepper.
3. In a small bowl, mix together the mustard, olive oil, honey, smoked paprika, and garlic powder.
4. Brush the mustard mixture over the pork chops, making sure to coat both sides.
5. Sprinkle breadcrumbs over the pork chops, pressing them down gently to adhere.
6. Place the pork chops in the air fryer basket and cook for 12 minutes or until the internal temperature reaches 65°C.
7. Let the pork chops rest for 5 minutes before serving.

Per serving:

Calories: 310, Fat: 17g, Protein: 25g, Carbohydrates: 9g Sodium:474mg Fibre: 0g

Honey Garlic Pork Chops

Serves 4,

Cooking time: 20 minutes

Ingredients:

- 4 bone-in pork chops (each about 200g)
- 2 cloves garlic, minced
- 2 tablespoons honey
- 2 tablespoons soy sauce
- 1 tablespoon olive oil
- 1/2 teaspoon ground ginger
- Salt and pepper, to taste

Instructions:

1. Preheat the air fryer to 200°C.
2. Pat the pork chops dry with paper towels and season with salt and pepper.
3. In a small bowl, whisk together the garlic, honey, soy sauce, olive oil, and ginger.
4. Brush the mixture over both sides of the pork chops.
5. Place the pork chops in the air fryer basket and cook for 10 minutes.
6. Flip the pork chops and cook for another 8-10 minutes, until the internal temperature reaches 63°C.
7. Remove the pork chops from the air fryer and let them rest for a few minutes before serving.

Per serving:

Calories: 315, Fat: 14g, Protein: 35g, Carbohydrates: 9g Sodium:362mg Fibre: 3g

Air Fryer Pork Meatballs

Serves 4

Cooking time: 15 mins

Ingredients:

- 500g pork mince
- 50g almond flour
- 1 egg

- 40 g finely chopped onion
- 2 cloves garlic, minced
- 1/2 tsp dried basil
- 1/2 tsp dried oregano
- 1/2 tsp salt
- 1/4 tsp black pepper

Instructions:

1. In a mixing bowl, combine pork mince, almond flour, egg, onion, garlic, basil, oregano, salt, and pepper. Mix until well combined.
2. Form the mixture into small meatballs, about 3 - 4 cm in diameter.
3. Preheat your air fryer to 200°C.
4. Place the meatballs in the air fryer basket in a single layer, making sure they do not touch each other.
5. Cook the meatballs in the air fryer for 12-15 minutes or until fully cooked, flipping them halfway through the Cooking time.
6. Once cooked, remove the meatballs from the air fryer and let them cool for a few minutes before serving.

Per serving:

Calories: 292, Fat: 22g, Protein: 20g, Carbohydrates: 4g Sodium:240mg Fibre: 2g

Air Fryer Lamb Chops with Garlic and Rosemary

Serves: 2

Cooking time: 10 minutes

Ingredients:

- 4 lamb chops
- 1 tbsp olive oil
- 2 cloves garlic, minced
- 1 tsp fresh rosemary, chopped
- Salt and pepper to taste

Instructions:

1. Preheat air fryer to 200°C.
2. In a small bowl, mix together olive oil, garlic, and rosemary.
3. Brush the mixture over both sides of the lamb chops and season with salt and pepper.
4. Place the lamb chops in the air fryer basket and cook for 8-10 minutes, flipping halfway through.

Per serving:

Calories: 300, Fat: 20g, Protein: 26g, Carbohydrates: 0g Sodium:240mg Fibre: 3g

Greek-Style Lamb Kabobs with Tzatziki

Serves: 4

Cooking time: 15 minutes

Ingredients:

- 455 g lamb, cut into 2.5 cm cubes
- 1 tbsp olive oil
- 1 tsp dried oregano
- Salt and pepper to taste
- Tzatziki sauce for serving

Instructions:

1. Preheat air fryer to 200°C.
2. In a small bowl, mix together olive oil, oregano, salt, and pepper.
3. Thread lamb cubes onto skewers and brush with the olive oil mixture.
4. Place the skewers in the air fryer basket and cook for 10-12 minutes, flipping halfway through.
5. Serve with tzatziki sauce.

Per serving:

Calories: 250, Carbohydrates: 2g Protein: 22g Fat:24g Sodium:210mg Fibre: 1g

Air Fryer Lamb Kofta

Serves: 4

Cooking time: 12 minutes

Ingredients:

- 455 g lamb mince
- 1/2 onion, grated
- 2 cloves garlic, minced
- 2 tbsp fresh parsley, chopped
- 2 tbsp fresh mint, chopped
- 1 tsp ground cumin
- 1 tsp ground coriander
- Salt and pepper to taste

Instructions:

1. Preheat air fryer to 190°C.
2. In a large bowl, mix together lamb, onion, garlic, parsley, mint, cumin, coriander, salt, and pepper.
3. Form the mixture into small, cylindrical meatballs.
4. Place the meatballs in the air fryer basket and cook for 10-12 minutes, shaking the basket halfway through.

Per serving:

Calories: 300, Carbohydrates: 2g Protein: 18g Fat:24g Sodium:210mg Fibre: 1g

Moroccan-Spiced Air Fryer Lamb Chops

Serves: 2

Cooking time: 12 minutes

Ingredients:

- 4 lamb chops
- 1 tbsp olive oil
- 1 tsp ground cumin
- 1 tsp ground coriander
- 1 tsp ground cinnamon
- Salt and pepper to taste

Instructions:

1. Preheat air fryer to 200°C.
2. In a small bowl, mix together olive oil, cumin, coriander, cinnamon, salt, and pepper.
3. Brush the mixture over both sides of the lamb chops.
4. Place the lamb chops in the air fryer basket and cook for 10-12 minutes, flipping halfway through.

Per serving:

Calories: 318 Carbohydrates: 1g Protein: 27g Fat:8g Sodium:231mg Fibre: 0g

Air Fryer Greek Lamb Chops

Servings: 4

Cooking time: 15 minutes

Ingredients:

- 8 lamb chops
- 2 tbsp olive oil
- 2 tbsp lemon juice
- 1 tsp dried oregano
- 1 tsp dried thyme
- 1/2 tsp garlic powder
- 1/2 tsp onion powder
- Salt and pepper, to taste

Instructions:

1. Preheat the air fryer to 200°C.
2. In a bowl, mix together the olive oil, lemon juice, oregano, thyme, garlic powder, onion powder, salt, and pepper.
3. Rub the mixture over the lamb chops, making sure to coat them well.
4. Place the lamb chops in the air fryer basket and cook for 10-15 minutes, flipping halfway through, until the internal temperature reaches 60°C for medium-rare.
5. Remove the lamb chops from the air fryer and let them rest for a few minutes before serving.

Per serving:
Calories: 295 Carbohydrates: 1g Protein: 24g Fat:22g Sodium:95mg Fibre: 0g

Air Fryer Moroccan Lamb Meatballs

Servings: 4

Cooking time: 15 minutes

Ingredients:
- 500g lamb mince
- 25 g breadcrumbs
- 25 g finely chopped onion
- 2 cloves garlic, minced
- 2 tbsp chopped fresh parsley
- 1 tbsp ground cumin
- 1 tsp paprika
- 1 tsp ground cinnamon
- 1/2 tsp ground coriander
- 1/2 tsp salt
- 1/4 tsp ground black pepper
- 1 egg
- Olive oil spray

Instructions:
1. In a large bowl, mix together the lamb, breadcrumbs, onion, garlic, parsley, cumin, paprika, cinnamon, coriander, salt, pepper, and egg.
2. Using your hands, shape the mixture into meatballs, making about 12.
3. Preheat the air fryer to 200°C.
4. Lightly spray the meatballs with olive oil spray and place them in the air fryer basket.
5. Cook for 10-15 minutes, until the internal temperature reaches 70°C.
6. Serve with your choice of dipping sauce or sides.

Per serving:
Calories: 325 Carbohydrates: 5g Protein: 20g Fat:25g Sodium:440mg Fibre: 1g

Air Fryer Beef and Vegetable Kabobs

Serves:4

Cooking time:8 - 10 mins

Ingredients:
- 400g beef sirloin steak, cut into cubes
- 1 red pepper, cut into large pieces
- 1 green pepper, cut into large pieces
- 1 red onion, cut into large pieces
- 8-10 cherry tomatoes
- 2 tbsp olive oil
- 2 garlic cloves, minced
- 1 tsp paprika
- 1 tsp cumin
- Salt and pepper, to taste

Instructions:
1. Preheat the air fryer to 180°C.
2. In a small bowl, combine olive oil, garlic, paprika, cumin, salt, and pepper.
3. Thread the beef, bell peppers, onion, and cherry tomatoes onto skewers.
4. Brush the kabobs with the olive oil mixture.
5. Place the skewers in the air fryer basket and cook for 8-10 minutes, flipping halfway through.

Per serving:
Calories: 290 Carbohydrates: 8g Protein: 27g Fat:16g Sodium:80mg Fibre: 2g

Air Fryer Beef Fajitas

Serves: 3-4

Cooking time:8 - 10 mins

Ingredients:
- 400g beef sirloin, thinly sliced
- 1 red pepper, thinly sliced
- 1 green pepper, thinly sliced
- 1 yellow onion, thinly sliced

- 2 tbsp olive oil
- 2 garlic cloves, minced
- 1 tsp cumin
- 1 tsp chili powder
- Salt and pepper, to taste
- 8 low-carb tortillas

Instructions:

1. Preheat the air fryer to 180°C.
2. In a small bowl, combine olive oil, garlic, cumin, chili powder, salt, and pepper.
3. Add the beef, bell peppers, and onion to the bowl and toss to coat.
4. Place the beef mixture in the air fryer basket and cook for 8-10 minutes, shaking the basket halfway through.
5. Serve with low-carb tortillas.

Per serving:

Calories: 330 Carbohydrates: 18g Protein: 30g Fat:14g Sodium:420mg Fibre: 3g

Air Fryer Steak

Serves: 4

Cooking time: 8-10 mins

Ingredients:

- 500g sirloin steak
- 2 tbsp olive oil
- 2 garlic cloves, minced
- 1 tsp paprika
- Salt and pepper, to taste

Instructions:

1. Preheat the air fryer to 200°C.
2. In a small bowl, combine olive oil, garlic, paprika, salt, and pepper.
3. Rub the olive oil mixture all over the steak.
4. Place the steak in the air fryer basket and cook for 8-10 minutes, flipping halfway through.
5. Let the steak rest for 5 minutes before slicing and serving.

Per serving:

Calories: 400 Carbohydrates: 1g Protein: 37g Fat:26g Sodium:150mg Fibre: 0g

Air Fryer Beef Jerky

Serves: 4

Cooking time: 4-6 hours

Ingredients:

- 500 grams beef (sirloin, flank steak, or round steak)
- 2 tablespoons soy sauce
- 2 tablespoons Worcestershire sauce
- 1 tablespoon honey
- 1 teaspoon garlic powder
- 1 teaspoon onion powder
- 1/2 teaspoon black pepper
- 1/2 teaspoon smoked paprika

Instructions:

1. Cut the beef into thin slices, about ¼ cm thick.
2. In a small bowl, mix together the soy sauce, Worcestershire sauce, honey, garlic powder, onion powder, black pepper, and smoked paprika.
3. Add the beef slices to the marinade, making sure each piece is coated. Cover the bowl with plastic wrap and refrigerate for at least 1 hour, or up to overnight.
4. Preheat the air fryer to 160°C.
5. Remove the beef slices from the marinade and pat them dry with paper towels.
6. Arrange the beef slices in a single layer in the air fryer basket, making sure they are not touching.
7. Air fry for 4-6 hours, or until the beef jerky is dry and chewy. Check on the jerky every hour and flip the pieces over to ensure even cooking.
8. Once done, remove the beef jerky from the

air fryer and let it cool completely before storing in an airtight container.

Per serving (25 g):

Calories: 90 Carbohydrates: 2g Protein: 10g Fat: 5g Cholesterol: 89mg Sodium:270mg Fibre: 0g

Air Fryer Beef Kofta

Serves 4

Cooking time: 15-17 mins

Ingredients:

- 500g lean beef mince
- 1 small onion, grated
- 2 garlic cloves, minced
- 1 tsp ground cumin
- 1 tsp ground coriander
- 1/2 tsp paprika
- 1/4 tsp ground cinnamon
- 1/4 tsp ground allspice
- 1/4 tsp ground nutmeg
- Salt and pepper, to taste
- Cooking spray

Instructions:

1. In a large bowl, mix together beef, grated onion, minced garlic, ground cumin, ground coriander, paprika, ground cinnamon, ground allspice, ground nutmeg, salt and pepper.
2. Form the mixture into 12 sausage-shaped koftas.
3. Preheat your air fryer to 190°C.
4. Spray the air fryer basket with cooking spray and place the koftas in the basket, making sure they are not touching.
5. Cook for 10 minutes, then flip the koftas and cook for another 5-7 minutes until cooked through.
6. Serve hot with a side salad or tzatziki sauce.

Per serving:

Calories: 230 Carbohydrates: 3g Protein: 29g Fat: 11g Cholesterol: 89mg Sodium:131mg Fibre: 1g

Air Fryer Asian Beef Skewers

Serves 4

Cooking time: 10-12 mins

Ingredients:

- 500g beef sirloin, sliced into thin strips
- 60 ml soy sauce
- 2 tablespoons honey
- 2 tablespoons rice vinegar
- 2 tablespoons sesame oil
- 2 teaspoons minced garlic
- 1 teaspoon grated ginger
- 1/2 teaspoon red pepper flakes
- 1/4 teaspoon black pepper
- 30 g chopped spring onions

Instructions:

1. In a large bowl, whisk together the soy sauce, honey, rice vinegar, sesame oil, garlic, ginger, red pepper flakes, and black pepper.
2. Add the beef strips to the bowl and toss to coat evenly.
3. Cover the bowl with plastic wrap and refrigerate for at least 1 hour (or up to 4 hours) to marinate.
4. When ready to cook, preheat the air fryer to 200°C.
5. Thread the beef strips onto skewers.
6. Place the skewers in the air fryer basket and cook for 6-8 minutes, flipping halfway through.
7. Remove from the air fryer and sprinkle with chopped spring onions before serving.

Per serving:

Calories: 294 Carbohydrates: 11g Protein: 33g Fat: 12g Cholesterol: 94mg Sodium: 942mg Fibre: 1g

Chapter 6 Vegetable Recipes

Air Fryer Crispy Tofu

Serves 4,

Cooking time: 20 minutes

Ingredients:
- 400g firm tofu, drained and pressed
- 2 tbsp cornflour
- 1 tsp smoked paprika
- 1 tsp garlic powder
- 1/2 tsp salt
- 1/4 tsp black pepper
- Cooking spray

Instructions:
1. Preheat the air fryer to 200°C.
2. Cut the tofu into small cubes.
3. In a small bowl, mix together the cornflour, smoked paprika, garlic powder, salt and black pepper.
4. Toss the tofu in the spice mixture until evenly coated.
5. Spray the air fryer basket with cooking spray.
6. Arrange the tofu in a single layer in the air fryer basket.
7. Cook for 10 minutes, then flip the tofu and cook for another 10 minutes until golden and crispy.
8. Serve hot with your favourite dipping sauce.

Per serving:
Calories:136 Carbohydrates: 8g Protein: 13g Fat:6g Sodium: 305mg Fiber: 1g

Roasted Cauliflower Steaks

Serves 4,

Cook time: 25 minutes

Ingredients:
- 1 head of cauliflower
- 3 tablespoons olive oil
- 2 teaspoons smoked paprika
- 1/2 teaspoon salt
- 1/4 teaspoon black pepper

Instructions:
1. Preheat the air fryer to 200°C.
2. Cut the cauliflower into 2.5 cm thick slices, discarding the stem and leaves.
3. In a small bowl, mix together the olive oil, smoked paprika, salt, and black pepper.
4. Brush the cauliflower slices with the oil mixture on both sides.
5. Place the cauliflower slices in the air fryer basket in a single layer.
6. Air fry for 12-15 minutes, flipping once halfway through cooking, until the cauliflower is tender and golden brown.
7. Serve immediately.

Per serving:
Calories:105 Carbohydrates: 6g Protein: 3g Fat:9g Sodium: 222mg Fiber: 3g

Vegetable Fajitas

Serves 4,

Cooking time: 15 minutes

Ingredients:
- 2 peppers, sliced
- 1 onion, sliced
- 2 courgettes, sliced
- 1 tablespoon olive oil
- 1 teaspoon cumin
- 1 teaspoon chili powder
- 1/2 teaspoon paprika
- Salt and pepper, to taste
- 4 whole wheat tortillas
- Salsa and guacamole, for serving

Instructions:

1. Preheat the air fryer to 200°C.
2. In a bowl, combine the sliced peppers, onion, and courgette. Drizzle with olive oil and sprinkle with cumin, chili powder, paprika, salt, and pepper. Toss to combine.
3. Add the vegetables to the air fryer basket and cook for 10-12 minutes, shaking the basket every 5 minutes, until the vegetables are tender and lightly charred.
4. While the vegetables are cooking, warm the tortillas in the microwave or on a frying pan.
5. To serve, divide the vegetables among the tortillas and top with salsa and guacamole.

Per serving:

Calories: 207 Carbohydrates: 35g Protein: 6g Fat:6g Sodium: 200mg Fiber: 8g

Air Fryer Sweet Potato Fries

Serves 4,

Cooking time: 20 minutes

Ingredients:

- 2 large sweet potatoes, peeled and cut into fries
- 2 tbsp olive oil
- 1 tsp garlic powder
- 1 tsp smoked paprika
- Salt and pepper to taste

Instructions:

1. Preheat the air fryer to 200°C.
2. In a mixing bowl, combine sweet potato fries, olive oil, garlic powder, smoked paprika, salt, and pepper.
3. Toss the fries until they are well coated.
4. Place the fries in the air fryer basket in a single layer.
5. Cook for 15-20 minutes, shaking the basket halfway through, or until the fries are crispy and golden brown.

Per serving:

Calories: 180 Carbohydrates: 28g Protein: 2g Fat: 7g Sodium: 215mg Fiber: 4g

Baked Sweet Potato Falafel

Serves 4,

Cook time 25 minutes

- 400g canned chickpeas, drained and rinsed
- 400g sweet potato, peeled and grated
- 50g plain flour
- 1 small onion, chopped
- 2 garlic cloves, minced
- 1 tbsp ground cumin
- 1 tbsp ground coriander
- 1 tsp smoked paprika
- 1 tsp salt
- 2 tbsp olive oil
- For the sauce:
- 150g Greek yoghurt
- 1 garlic clove, minced
- Juice of 1/2 lemon
- Salt and pepper to taste

Instructions:

1. Preheat the air fryer to 180°C.
2. In a food processor, combine the chickpeas, grated sweet potato, plain flour, onion, garlic, cumin, coriander, paprika, and salt. Pulse until well combined.
3. Using your hands, shape the mixture into small balls.
4. Brush the falafel balls with olive oil.
5. Place the falafel balls in the air fryer basket and cook for 12-15 minutes, turning halfway through, until golden brown and crispy.
6. While the falafel cooks, mix together the Greek yoghurt, garlic, lemon juice, salt and pepper in a small bowl.
7. Serve the hot falafel with the sauce on the side.

Per serving (including sauce):

Calories: 319 Carbohydrates: 43g Protein: 13g Fat: 11g Sodium: 398mg Fiber: 10g

Courgette Fritters

Serves 4,

Cook time 12 minutes

- 2 medium courgettes (zucchini), grated
- 60g all-purpose flour
- 1/2 tsp baking powder
- 1/2 tsp salt
- 1/4 tsp black pepper
- 1/4 tsp garlic powder
- 2 large eggs, lightly beaten
- 50g grated cheddar cheese
- 1 tbsp chopped fresh parsley
- 1 tbsp olive oil

Instructions:

1. Preheat the air fryer to 190°C.
2. In a mixing bowl, combine the grated courgettes, all-purpose flour, baking powder, salt, black pepper, and garlic powder. Mix well.
3. Add the lightly beaten eggs, grated cheddar cheese, and chopped fresh parsley to the bowl. Mix until well combined.
4. Using a tablespoon, scoop the mixture into the air fryer basket, leaving some space between each fritter.
5. Brush the tops of the fritters with olive oil.
6. Cook for 8-10 minutes, or until the fritters are golden brown and crispy.
7. Serve hot

Per serving:

Calories: 169 Carbohydrates: 12g Protein: 9g Fat: 10g Cholesterol: 105mg Sodium: 497mg Fiber: 1g

Roasted Vegetables

Serves 4,

Cooking time: 20 minutes

Ingredients:

- 500g mixed vegetables (e.g. broccoli, cauliflower, peppers, courgette, etc.), cut into bite-sized pieces
- 1 tablespoon olive oil
- 1/2 teaspoon salt
- 1/2 teaspoon garlic powder
- 1/4 teaspoon black pepper
- Cooking spray

Instructions:

1. Preheat the air fryer to 200°C.
2. In a bowl, toss the vegetables with olive oil, salt, garlic powder, and black pepper.
3. Spray the air fryer basket with cooking spray.
4. Arrange the vegetables in a single layer in the basket.
5. Air fry for 10 minutes, then shake the basket and air fry for another 5-10 minutes, until the vegetables are tender and golden brown.
6. Serve as a side dish or over a bed of rice or quinoa.

Per serving:

Calories: 90 Carbohydrates: 12g Protein: 4g Fat: 4g Sodium: 325mg Fiber: 4g

Roasted Brussels Sprouts and Sweet Potatoes

Serves 4,

Cooking time: 25 minutes

Ingredients:

- 500g Brussels sprouts, trimmed and halved
- 500g sweet potatoes, peeled and cubed
- 2 tbsp olive oil
- 1 tsp garlic powder
- 1 tsp paprika
- Salt and pepper, to taste

Instructions:

1. Preheat the air fryer to 200°C.

2. In a large bowl, combine the Brussels sprouts and sweet potatoes.
3. Drizzle the olive oil over the vegetables and toss to coat.
4. Add the garlic powder, paprika, salt, and pepper, and toss again until the vegetables are evenly coated with the seasoning.
5. Place the vegetables in the air fryer basket, spreading them out in a single layer.
6. Air fry for 15-20 minutes, shaking the basket occasionally, until the vegetables are tender and browned.
7. Serve hot.

Per serving:
Calories: 197 Carbohydrates: 32g Protein: 6g Fat: 7g Sodium: 97mg Fiber: 8g

Stuffed Portobello Mushrooms

Serves 4,

Cooking time: 20 minutes

Ingredients:
- 4 large portobello mushrooms, stems removed
- 90g cooked quinoa
- 25g diced onion
- 25g diced red bell pepper
- 2 cloves garlic, minced
- 1/2 tsp dried oregano
- 1/4 tsp salt
- 1/4 tsp black pepper
- 30g crumbled feta cheese
- 20g grated Parmesan cheese
- 2 tbsp chopped fresh parsley
- 1 tbsp olive oil

Instructions:
1. Preheat air fryer to 190°C.
2. Remove the stems from the portobello mushrooms and discard them.
3. In a mixing bowl, combine the cooked quinoa, diced onion, diced red bell pepper, minced garlic, dried oregano, salt, black pepper, crumbled feta cheese, grated Parmesan cheese, and chopped fresh parsley. Mix well.
4. Brush the mushroom caps with olive oil on both sides.
5. Stuff each mushroom cap with the quinoa mixture, pressing down gently to fill the cap.
6. Place the stuffed mushroom caps in the air fryer basket.
7. Cook for 10-12 minutes, or until the mushrooms are tender and the filling is heated through.

Serve hot.

Per serving:
Calories: 122 Carbohydrates: 10g Protein: 6g Fat: 7g Cholesterol: 13mg Sodium: 302mg Fiber: 2g

Air Fryer Veggie Burger

Serves 4,

Cooking time: 20 minutes

Ingredients:
- 1 can chickpeas, drained and rinsed
- 90g cooked quinoa
- 50g breadcrumbs
- 50g grated carrot
- 25g diced onion
- 25g diced celery
- 2 cloves garlic, minced
- 1 tsp cumin
- 1/2 tsp smoked paprika
- 1/4 tsp salt
- 1/4 tsp black pepper
- 1 egg, beaten
- 1 tbsp olive oil
- 4 burger buns
- lettuce, tomato, and other desired toppings

Instructions:

1. Preheat air fryer to 190°C.
2. In a food processor, pulse chickpeas, onion, garlic, red pepper, courgette, rolled oats, olive oil, paprika, salt, and pepper until combined but still slightly chunky.
3. Divide the mixture into four equal parts and shape into burger patties.
4. Place the patties in the air fryer basket and cook for 10 minutes, flipping halfway through.
5. Serve hot on buns with your favourite toppings.

Per serving:

Calories: 379 Carbohydrates: 53g Protein: 14g Fat: 12g Cholesterol: 47mg Sodium: 635mg Fiber: 9g

Air Fryer Tofu and Broccoli

Serves 2,

Cooking time: 20 minutes

Ingredients:

- 1 block firm tofu (350g), drained and pressed
- 1 head of broccoli, cut into small florets (250g)
- 2 tbsp cornstarch
- 1/2 tsp garlic powder
- 1/4 tsp onion powder
- 1/4 tsp paprika
- 1/4 tsp salt
- 1/8 tsp black pepper
- 1 tbsp olive oil

Instructions:

1. Cut the tofu into small cubes.
2. In a bowl, mix together the cornstarch, garlic powder, onion powder, paprika, salt, and black pepper.
3. Add the tofu cubes to the bowl and toss them in the cornstarch mixture until they are coated.
4. Preheat the air fryer to 375°F (190°C).
5. Place the tofu cubes in the air fryer basket, leaving a little space between each one.
6. Cook the tofu for 10 minutes, then flip them over.
7. Add the broccoli florets to the air fryer basket and drizzle them with olive oil.
8. Cook for another 10 minutes, or until the tofu is crispy and the broccoli is tender.
9. Serve hot as a main dish or over a bed of rice.

Per serving:

Calories: 309 Carbohydrates: 21g Protein: 20g Fat: 18g Cholesterol: 0mg Sodium: 463mg Fiber: 6g

Roasted Brussel Sprouts

Serves 4,

Cooking time 20 minutes

Ingredients:

- 500g Brussel sprouts, trimmed and halved
- 2 tbsp olive oil
- 1/2 tsp salt
- 1/4 tsp black pepper
- 1/4 tsp garlic powder
- 1/4 tsp onion powder

Instructions:

1. Preheat the air fryer to 180°C.
2. In a mixing bowl, combine the Brussel sprouts, olive oil, salt, pepper, garlic powder, and onion powder. Mix well.
3. Place the seasoned Brussel sprouts into the air fryer basket.
4. Cook for 15-20 minutes or until the sprouts are crispy on the outside and tender on the inside.

Per serving:

Calories:100 Carbohydrates:9g Protein:3g Fat:7g Cholesterol: 0mg Sodium:318mg
- Fiber: 4g

Garlic Roasted Carrots

Serves 4

Cooking time 20 minutes

Ingredients:

- 500g carrots, peeled and sliced
- 2 tbsp olive oil
- 3 cloves garlic, minced
- 1/2 tsp salt
- 1/4 tsp black pepper
- 1 tbsp chopped fresh parsley

Instructions:

1. Preheat the air fryer to 180°C.
2. In a mixing bowl, combine the carrots, olive oil, garlic, salt, and pepper. Mix well.
3. Place the seasoned carrots into the air fryer basket.
4. Cook for 15-20 minutes or until the carrots are tender and lightly browned.
5. Sprinkle with chopped parsley before serving.

Per serving:

Calories:94 Carbohydrates:8g Protein:1g Fat:7g Cholesterol: 0mg Sodium:356mg , Fiber: 3g

Air Fryer Asparagus

Serves 4

Cooking time 10 minutes

Ingredients:

- 500g asparagus, trimmed
- 2 tbsp olive oil
- 1/2 tsp salt
- 1/4 tsp black pepper
- 1/2 tsp garlic powder
- 1/2 tsp onion powder

Instructions:

1. Preheat the air fryer to 200°C.
2. In a mixing bowl, combine the asparagus, olive oil, salt, pepper, garlic powder, and onion powder. Mix well.
3. Place the seasoned asparagus into the air fryer basket.
4. Cook for 8-10 minutes or until the asparagus is tender and slightly crispy.

Per serving:

Calories:68 Carbohydrates:5g Protein:2g Fat:5g Cholesterol: 0mg Sodium:336mg, Fiber: 3g

Air Fryer Green Beans

Serves 4,

Cooking time: 15 minutes

Ingredients:

- 500g green beans, trimmed
- 2 tbsp olive oil
- 1 tsp sea salt
- 1/2 tsp black pepper
- 1/2 tsp garlic powder

Instructions:

1. Preheat air fryer to 180°C.
2. In a mixing bowl, combine the green beans, olive oil, salt, pepper, and garlic powder. Toss until the green beans are coated.
3. Place the green beans in the air fryer basket and cook for 10-15 minutes, shaking the basket occasionally to ensure even cooking.
4. Serve hot.

Per serving:

Calories:70 Carbohydrates:9g Protein:2g Fat:4g Cholesterol: 0mg Sodium: 590mg , Fiber: 4g

Air Fryer Veggie Skewers

Serves 4

Cooking time: 15 minutes

Ingredients:
- 1 red onion, cut into chunks (2cm x 2cm)
- 1 red pepper, cut into chunks (2cm x 2cm)
- 1 green pepper, cut into chunks (2cm x 2cm)
- 1 courgette, cut into rounds (2cm thick)
- 8 cherry tomatoes
- 1 tablespoon olive oil
- 1 teaspoon dried oregano
- Salt and pepper, to taste

Instructions:
1. Preheat the air fryer to 200°C.
2. Thread the vegetables onto skewers, alternating the different vegetables.
3. In a small bowl, mix the olive oil, dried oregano, salt, and pepper.
4. Brush the mixture over the skewered vegetables.
5. Place the skewers in the air fryer basket and cook for 15 minutes or until the vegetables are cooked to your liking.
6. Serve hot.

Per serving:
Calories:77 Carbohydrates:10g Protein:2g Fat:4g Cholesterol: 0mg Sodium: 8mg , Fiber: 3g

Stuffed Courgettes

Servings: 2

Cooking time: 20 minutes

Ingredients:
- 2 medium courgettes (400g)
- 90g cooked quinoa
- 30g chopped mushrooms
- 30g chopped red pepper
- 15g chopped onion
- 7.5ml olive oil
- 1/2 teaspoon dried oregano
- 1/2 teaspoon paprika
- 1/4 teaspoon salt
- 1/4 teaspoon black pepper

Instructions:
1. Preheat the airfryer to 180°C.
2. Cut off the tops of the courgettes and scoop out the seeds with a spoon.
3. In a mixing bowl, combine the cooked quinoa, mushrooms, red pepper, onion, olive oil, oregano, paprika, salt, and black pepper.
4. Stuff the courgettes with the quinoa mixture.
5. Place the stuffed courgettes in the airfryer basket and cook for 20 minutes.
6. Serve hot.

Per serving:
Calories:154 Carbohydrates:18g Protein:5g Fat:7g Cholesterol: 0mg Sodium: 305mg , Fiber: 4g

Airfryer Garlic Mushrooms

Servings: 2

Cooking time: 10 minutes

Ingredients:
- 200g mushrooms, sliced
- 10g olive oil
- 1 garlic clove, minced
- 1/2 teaspoon dried thyme
- Salt and pepper, to taste

Instructions:
1. Preheat the airfryer to 180°C.
2. In a mixing bowl, combine the sliced mushrooms, olive oil, garlic, thyme, salt, and pepper.
3. Place the seasoned mushrooms in the airfryer basket.
4. Cook for 10 minutes, shaking the basket

halfway through.
5. Serve hot.

Per serving:

Calories: 67 Carbohydrates:3g Protein:2g Fat:5g Cholesterol: 0mg Sodium: 5mg , Fiber: 1g

Airfryer Herb Roasted Potatoes

Servings: 4

Cooking time: 20 minutes

Ingredients:

- 600g baby potatoes, halved
- 10g olive oil
- 1 teaspoon dried thyme
- 1/2 teaspoon dried rosemary
- Salt and pepper, to taste

Instructions:

1. Preheat the airfryer to 200°C.
2. In a mixing bowl, combine the halved baby potatoes, olive oil, dried thyme, dried rosemary, salt, and pepper.
3. Place the seasoned potatoes in the airfryer basket.
4. Cook for 20 minutes, shaking the basket halfway through.
5. Serve hot.

Per serving:

Calories: 125 Carbohydrates: 22g Protein:3g Fat:3g Cholesterol: 0mg Sodium: 6mg , Fiber: 3g

Airfryer Baked Potatoes

Servings: 2

Cooking time: 30 minutes

Ingredients:

- 2 medium-sized potatoes, washed and dried
- 5g olive oil
- Salt and pepper, to taste

Instructions:

1. Preheat the airfryer to 180°C.
2. Rub each potato with a small amount of olive oil and season with salt and pepper.
3. Pierce each potato several times with a fork.
4. Place the potatoes in the airfryer basket.
5. Cook for 30 minutes, or until the potatoes are tender when pierced with a fork.
6. Serve hot with your choice of toppings, such as low-fat sour cream or chives.

Per serving:

Calories: 134 Carbohydrates: 26g Protein:3g Fat:3g Cholesterol: 0mg Sodium: 12mg , Fiber: 3g

Airfryer Classic Potato Fries

Servings: 4

Cooking time: 20 minutes

Ingredients:

- 600g potatoes, cut into ½ cm fries
- 5g olive oil
- Salt and pepper, to taste

Instructions:

1. Preheat the airfryer to 200°C.
2. In a mixing bowl, toss the potato fries with olive oil, salt, and pepper.
3. Place the seasoned potato fries in the airfryer basket.
4. Cook for 20 minutes, shaking the basket halfway through.
5. Serve hot with your favourite dipping sauce.

Per serving:

Calories: 126 Carbohydrates: 28g Protein:2g Fat:1g Cholesterol: 0mg Sodium: 9mg , Fiber: 3g

Chapter 7 Snacks and Appetisers

Airfryer Quinoa and Black Bean Cakes

Servings: 4

Cooking time: 20 minutes

Ingredients:
- 200g cooked quinoa
- 1 can black beans, drained and rinsed (400g)
- 1/2 red onion, chopped
- 1/2 red bell pepper, chopped
- 60g breadcrumbs
- 2 tbsp chopped fresh cilantro
- 1 tbsp ground cumin
- 1 tbsp chili powder
- 1 tsp garlic powder
- 1/2 tsp salt
- 1/4 tsp black pepper
- 2 tbsp olive oil

Instructions:
1. In a large mixing bowl, combine the cooked quinoa, black beans, chopped red onion, chopped red bell pepper, breadcrumbs, cilantro, cumin, chili powder, garlic powder, salt, and black pepper. Mix well.
2. Form the mixture into 8 evenly sized patties.
3. Preheat the air fryer to 375°F (190°C).
4. Brush the patties with olive oil on both sides.
5. Place the patties in the air fryer basket, leaving a little space between each one.
6. Cook the patties for 10 minutes, then flip them over.
7. Cook for another 10 minutes, or until the patties are crispy and golden brown.
8. Serve hot with your favorite dipping sauce or as a side dish.

Per serving:
Calories: 296 Carbohydrates: 42g Protein:11g Fat:8g Cholesterol: 0mg Sodium: 664mg , Fiber: 10g

Airfryer Crispy Kale

Servings: 4

Cooking time: 5-8 minutes

Ingredients:
- 1 bunch of kale, washed and dried (approx. 300g)
- 2 tablespoons of olive oil
- 1 teaspoon of garlic powder
- Salt and pepper, to taste

Instructions:
1. Preheat the airfryer to 180°C.
2. Remove the kale leaves from the thick stem, and tear into bite-size pieces.
3. In a large mixing bowl, toss the kale with olive oil, garlic powder, salt, and pepper.
4. Place the kale in the air fryer and cook for 5-8 minutes or until crispy and slightly charred, flipping halfway through.

Per serving:
Calories: 96 Carbohydrates: 7g Protein:3g Fat:7g Cholesterol: 0mg Sodium:51mg , Fiber: 2g

Airfryer Vegetable Pakoras

Servings: 4

Cooking time: 8-10 minutes

Ingredients:
- 250g gram flour
- 1 teaspoon of cumin powder
- 1 teaspoon of coriander powder
- 1 teaspoon of ginger powder
- 1/2 teaspoon of red chili powder

- Salt, to taste
- Water, as needed
- Oil, for brushing
- 250g mixed vegetables (such as onions, peppers, carrots, and cauliflower), cut into small pieces

Instructions:

1. Preheat the airfryer to 180°C.
2. In a large mixing bowl, combine the gram flour, cumin powder, coriander powder, ginger powder, red chili powder, and salt. Slowly add enough water to make a thick batter. The consistency should be thick enough to coat the vegetables.
3. Dip the vegetables into the batter, making sure they are well coated.
4. Place the battered vegetables in the air fryer and brush them with a little oil.
5. Cook for 8-10 minutes or until golden brown and crispy.
6. Remove from the air fryer and drain on a paper towel.
7. Serve hot with your favourite dipping sauce.

Per serving:

Calories: 312 Carbohydrates: 51g Protein:12g Fat:7g Cholesterol: 0mg Sodium:263mg , Fiber: 9g

Porridge Bread

Serves: 8

Cook time: 30 - 40 mins

Ingredients:

- 200 g rolled oats
- 350 ml water
- 5 g salt
- 3 g active dry yeast
- 25 g honey or maple syrup (optional, for sweetness)

Instructions:

1. In a medium-sized mixing bowl, combine the rolled oats, water, salt, and yeast. If you are using honey or maple syrup, add it now as well. Mix everything together until well combined.
2. Let the mixture sit at room temperature for at least 1 hour, or until it has doubled in size. The exact time will depend on the temperature and humidity in your kitchen, so you may need to adjust the time accordingly.
3. Preheat your air fryer to 190 °C.
4. Once the mixture has risen, use your hands to shape it into a loaf. You can either form it into a round shape or an oval shape, depending on your preference.
5. Place the loaf into the air fryer basket, making sure to leave enough space around it for the hot air to circulate.
6. Cook the bread for 30-40 minutes, or until it has formed a crust and sounds hollow when tapped on the bottom.
7. Remove the bread from the air fryer and allow it to cool for at least 15 minutes before slicing and serving.
8. The bread can be stored in a sealed container for up to 3 days at room temperature, or it can be frozen for later use.:

Per serving 1 slice (1/8th of the loaf):

Calories: 97 Carbohydrates: 18g Protein:3.1g Fat:2g Cholesterol: 0mg Sodium:576mg , Fiber: 2.6g

Fish Fingers

Serves: 4 - 6

Cooking time: 8 -10 mins

Ingredients:

- 500g white fish fillets, cut into finger-sized pieces

- 125g plain flour
- 1 teaspoon paprika
- 1 teaspoon garlic powder
- 1/2 teaspoon salt
- 1/4 teaspoon black pepper
- 2 eggs, beaten
- 125g breadcrumbs
- 30g grated Parmesan cheese

Instructions:

1. Preheat your air fryer to 180°C.
2. In a shallow dish, combine the flour, paprika, garlic powder, salt, and pepper.
3. In a separate shallow dish, beat the eggs.
4. In another shallow dish, mix together the breadcrumbs and grated Parmesan cheese.
5. Dip each fish finger in the flour mixture, then the beaten eggs, and finally the breadcrumb mixture, pressing the breadcrumbs onto the fish to adhere.
6. Place the fish fingers in the air fryer basket, making sure they are not overcrowded.
7. Cook the fish fingers for 8-10 minutes or until golden brown and cooked through.

Per serving:

Calories: 276 Carbohydrates: 31g Protein:24g Fat:6g Cholesterol: 99mg, Sodium:576mg Fiber: 1g

Cauliflower Buffalo Wings

Serves: 4

Cooking time: 25 mins

Ingredients:

- 1 head of cauliflower, cut into florets
- 60 g flour
- 1/2 teaspoon of garlic powder
- 1/2 teaspoon of onion powder
- Salt and pepper, to taste
- 120 ml hot sauce
- 2 tablespoons of butter, melted
- Blue cheese dressing, for dipping

Instructions:

1. Preheat the air fryer to 180 °C.
2. In a large mixing bowl, combine the flour, garlic powder, onion powder, salt, and pepper.
3. Dip the cauliflower florets in the flour mixture, making sure they are well coated.
4. Place the cauliflower florets in the air fryer and cook for 15-20 minutes or until tender and crispy.
5. Remove from the air fryer and toss in the hot sauce and melted butter.
6. Place the cauliflower florets back in the air fryer and cook for another 2-3 minutes.
7. Remove from the air fryer and serve with blue cheese dressing.

Per serving (Serves 4):

Calories: 159 Carbohydrates: 26g Protein: 5g Fat:6g Sodium:1190mg Fiber: 4g

Air Fryer Mozzarella Sticks

Prep time: 15 mins Cook time: 8 - 10 mins Serves: 4

Ingredients:

- 12 mozzarella sticks
- 125 g plain flour
- 1 tsp garlic powder
- 1 tsp onion powder
- 1/2 tsp salt
- 1/4 tsp black pepper
- 2 eggs, beaten
- 100 g seasoned breadcrumbs
- 2 tbsp grated Parmesan cheese
- Cooking spray

Instructions:

1. Preheat your air fryer to 200°C.
2. In a shallow dish, combine the flour, garlic

powder, onion powder, salt, and pepper.
3. In another shallow dish, beat the eggs.
4. In a third shallow dish, mix together the breadcrumbs and grated Parmesan cheese.
5. Dip each mozzarella stick in the flour mixture, then the beaten eggs, and finally the breadcrumb mixture, pressing the breadcrumbs onto the cheese to adhere.
6. Place the mozzarella sticks in the air fryer basket, making sure they are not overcrowded.
7. Spray the mozzarella sticks with cooking spray.
8. Cook the mozzarella sticks for 8-10 minutes or until golden brown and the cheese is melted.
9. Serve hot with your favourite dipping sauce.

Per serving:
Calories: 329 Carbohydrates: 26g Protein: 23g Fat:14g Sodium:928mg Fiber: 1g

Air Fryer Pita Chips

Cook time: 8 - 10 mins

Serves: 4

Ingredients:
- 2 whole wheat pita breads
- 1 tbsp olive oil
- 1 tsp garlic powder
- 1 tsp dried oregano
- Salt and black pepper, to taste

Instructions:
1. Preheat your air fryer to 180°C.
2. Cut the pita breads into wedges or bite-sized pieces.
3. In a small bowl, mix together the olive oil, garlic powder, dried oregano, salt, and black pepper.
4. Brush the pita bread pieces with the olive oil mixture.
5. Arrange the pita bread pieces in the air fryer basket, making sure they are not overcrowded.
6. Cook the pita bread pieces for 8-10 minutes or until golden brown and crispy.
7. Remove from the air fryer and let cool for a few minutes before serving.
8. Serve with your favourite dip or use as a topping for salads.

Per serving:
Calories: 80 Carbohydrates: 10g Protein: 3g Fat:4g Sodium:120mg Fiber: 2g

Crispy Brussels Sprouts Chips

Serves: 4

Cook time: 15 mins

Ingredients:
- 500g Brussels sprouts, trimmed and sliced thinly
- 1 tablespoon olive oil
- 1 teaspoon garlic powder
- 1 teaspoon onion powder
- 1/2 teaspoon salt
- 1/4 teaspoon black pepper

Instructions:
1. Preheat the air fryer to 190°C.
2. In a large mixing bowl, toss the Brussels sprouts with olive oil, garlic powder, onion powder, salt, and black pepper.
3. Place the seasoned Brussels sprouts in the air fryer basket and cook for 12-15 minutes, shaking the basket occasionally, until the chips are crispy and browned.
4. Serve immediately.

Per serving:
Calories: 104 Carbohydrates: 14.5g Protein: 6.9g Fat:0.6g Sodium:326mg Fiber: 6.6g

Air Fryer Vegetable Spring Rolls:

Serves: 4

Cook time: 10 mins

Ingredients:
- 8 spring roll wrappers
- 1 small carrot, grated
- 1 small red bell pepper, thinly sliced
- 1/2 small onion, thinly sliced
- 1 cup shredded cabbage
- 1 tsp garlic powder
- 1 tsp ground ginger
- 1 tbsp soy sauce
- 1 tbsp cornstarch
- 1 tbsp water
- Cooking spray

Instructions:
1. In a large bowl, mix together the grated carrot, sliced red bell pepper, thinly sliced onion, and shredded cabbage.
2. Add the garlic powder, ground ginger, and soy sauce to the bowl and stir until well combined.
3. In a small bowl, whisk together the cornstarch and water to create a slurry.
4. Lay out one spring roll wrapper and spoon 2-3 tablespoons of the vegetable mixture onto the bottom third of the wrapper.
5. Fold the sides of the wrapper over the filling and then roll it up tightly, tucking in the sides as you go.
6. Repeat the process with the remaining spring roll wrappers and vegetable mixture.
7. Preheat the air fryer to 200°C.
8. Spray the spring rolls with cooking spray on both sides.
9. Place the spring rolls in the air fryer basket and cook for 6 minutes.
10. Flip the spring rolls over and cook for another 6 minutes, or until they are crispy and golden brown.
11. Serve hot with your favorite dipping sauce.

Per serving:
Calories: 127 Carbohydrates: 27g Protein: 3g Fat:0g Sodium:434mg Fiber: 3g

Sweet Potato Tater Tots

Serves: 4

Cook time: 25 mins

Ingredients:
- 2 medium sweet potatoes, peeled and grated
- 60g panko breadcrumbs
- 25g grated parmesan cheese
- 1 tsp garlic powder
- 1/2 tsp salt
- 1/4 tsp black pepper
- 1 egg
- 1 tbsp olive oil

Instructions:
1. Preheat the oven to (220°C) and line a baking sheet with parchment paper.
2. Peel and grate the sweet potatoes using a box grater.
3. In a large bowl, mix together the grated sweet potatoes, panko breadcrumbs, parmesan cheese, garlic powder, salt, and black pepper.
4. Beat the egg in a small bowl and add it to the sweet potato mixture, stirring until well combined.
5. Using a small cookie scoop or spoon, form the mixture into small cylindrical shapes and place them onto the prepared baking sheet.
6. Brush the tater tots with olive oil.
7. Bake for 20-25 minutes, or until the tater tots are crispy and golden brown.
8. Serve hot with your favorite dipping sauce.

Per serving:
Calories: 170 Carbohydrates: 23g Protein: 6g Fat: 6g Cholesterol: 50mg Sodium: 420mg Fiber: 3g

Air Fryer Onion Rings:

Serves: 4

Cook time: 10 mins

Ingredients:
- 2 large onions, cut into rings
- 120g plain flour
- 2 tsp garlic powder
- 2 tsp onion powder
- 1 tsp paprika
- 1 tsp salt
- 1/2 tsp black pepper
- 2 eggs, beaten
- 120g breadcrumbs
- Cooking spray

Instructions:
1. Preheat your air fryer to 200°C.
2. In a shallow dish, mix together the flour, garlic powder, onion powder, paprika, salt, and pepper.
3. In another shallow dish, beat the eggs.
4. In a third shallow dish, mix together the breadcrumbs.
5. Dip each onion ring in the flour mixture, then the egg, and finally the breadcrumbs.
6. Spray the air fryer basket with cooking spray.
7. Place the onion rings in the air fryer basket, making sure they are not overcrowded.
8. Spray the onion rings with cooking spray.
9. Cook the onion rings for 8-10 minutes, flipping them halfway through, until they are golden brown and crispy.
10. Serve hot with your favourite dipping sauce.

Per serving:
Calories: 260 Carbohydrates:43g Protein:8g Fat:6g Cholesterol: 84mg Sodium:841mg , fibre: 3g

Air Fryer Chicken Sliders

Ingredients:
- 400g chicken mince
- 50g breadcrumbs
- 50g grated Parmesan cheese
- 1 tablespoon dried parsley
- 1 teaspoon garlic powder
- 1 teaspoon onion powder
- 1 teaspoon salt
- 1/2 teaspoon black pepper
- 8 small slider buns
- 8 slices of mozzarella cheese
- Marinara sauce and fresh basil, for serving

Instructions:
1. In a large mixing bowl, combine the chicken mince, breadcrumbs, grated Parmesan cheese, dried parsley, garlic powder, onion powder, salt, and black pepper. Mix well until all Ingredients are evenly combined.
2. Divide the mixture into 8 equal portions and shape each portion into a small burger.
3. Preheat the air fryer to 190°C.
4. Place the chicken burgers in the air fryer basket, making sure to leave enough space around each patty for air to circulate.
5. Cook the patties for 10-12 minutes or until fully cooked, flipping them over halfway through cooking.
6. While the patties are cooking, cut the slider buns in half and toast them in the air fryer for 1-2 minutes.
7. Assemble the sliders by placing a chicken burger on the bottom half of each bun, followed by a slice of mozzarella cheese, marinara sauce, and fresh basil.
8. Serve immediately.

Per serving (per slider):

Calories: 219 Carbohydrates:15g Protein:18g Fat:10g Sodium:576mg fibre: 1g

Air Fryer Sausage Rolls

Serves: 8

Cook time: 12-15 mins

Ingredients:

- 400g sausage meat
- 320g ready-rolled puff pastry
- 1 egg, beaten
- 1 tbsp sesame seeds (optional)
- Salt and pepper, to taste

Instructions:

1. Preheat your air fryer to 200°C.
2. Unroll the puff pastry and cut it in half lengthwise, then cut each half into four equal rectangles.
3. Divide the sausage meat into eight equal portions and roll each portion into a long sausage shape.
4. Place each sausage on a rectangle of puff pastry and brush the edges of the pastry with the beaten egg.
5. Fold the pastry over the sausage and press the edges together to seal. Cut each roll into four equal pieces.
6. Brush the tops of the sausage rolls with the remaining beaten egg and sprinkle with sesame seeds, if using.
7. Place the sausage rolls in the air fryer basket, leaving space between them for the hot air to circulate.
8. Cook for 12-15 minutes, or until the pastry is golden brown and the sausage is cooked through.
9. Remove from the air fryer and allow to cool slightly before serving.

Per serving:

Calories: 323 Carbohydrates:16g Protein:11g Fat:24g Cholesterol:63 mg Sodium:416mg fibre: 1g

Air Fryer 'Roasted' Peppers

Serves: 4-6

Cook time: 8-10 mins

Ingredients:

- 400g peppers, seeded and sliced
- 2 tbsp olive oil
- 1 tsp smoked paprika
- Salt and pepper, to taste

Instructions:

1. Preheat the air fryer to 180°C.
2. In a large mixing bowl, toss the sliced peppers with olive oil, smoked paprika, salt, and pepper.
3. Place the seasoned peppers in the air fryer basket and spread them out in a single layer.
4. Cook the peppers in the air fryer for 8-10 minutes, flipping them halfway through, until they are tender and slightly charred.
5. Serve the 'roasted' peppers hot as a side dish or use them in other recipes like sandwiches, wraps, salads, or pasta dishes.

Per serving (1/6 of recipe):

Calories: 65 Carbohydrates:5g Protein:1g Fat:5g Cholesterol:0 mg Sodium:1mg , fibre: 1g

Tuna Melt

Serves: 2

Cook time: 3-5 mins

Ingredients:

- 200g canned tuna in water, drained
- 100g diced celery

- 100g diced onion
- 2 tablespoons of light mayonnaise
- 100g reduced-fat cheddar cheese, grated
- Salt and pepper, to taste
- 2 slices of whole grain bread

Instructions:

1. Preheat the air fryer to 180 °C.
2. In a mixing bowl, combine the canned tuna, diced celery, onion, light mayonnaise, salt, and pepper. Mix until well combined.
3. Spread the tuna mixture on one slice of whole grain bread, top with grated cheese and another slice of bread to make a sandwich.
4. Place the sandwich in the air fryer and cook for 3-5 minutes or until the bread is golden brown and the cheese is melted, flipping halfway through.
5. Serve with a side salad or veggies for a complete meal.

Per serving (1 tuna melt):

Calories: 272   Carbohydrates:17g   Protein:23g
Fat:11g   Cholesterol:47 mg   Sodium: 540mg
fibre: 3g

Calzone

Serves: 1-2

Cook time: 10-12 mins

Ingredients:

- 1 batch of homemade or ready-made whole wheat pizza dough
- 100g of low-fat ricotta cheese
- 100g of turkey pepperoni or diced cooked chicken breast
- 100g of low fat mozzarella cheese, shredded
- 2 tablespoons of olive oil
- 1 teaspoon of dried oregano
- 1/2 teaspoon of garlic powder
- Salt and pepper, to taste

Instructions:

1. Preheat the air fryer to 180°C.
2. Roll out the pizza dough into a large circle, about 1/2 cm thick.
3. In a mixing bowl, combine the ricotta cheese, pepperoni or cooked chicken, mozzarella cheese, dried oregano, garlic powder, salt, and pepper. Mix until well combined.
4. Spread the mixture over half of the rolled-out dough, leaving a 2.5 cm border around the edge.
5. Fold the other half of the dough over the filling and press the edges together to seal.
6. Brush the top of the calzone with olive oil.
7. Place the calzone in the air fryer and cook for 10-12 minutes or until the crust is golden brown and the filling is hot.

Per serving:

Calories: 414   Carbohydrates:38g   Protein:28g
Fat:18g   Cholesterol:40 mg   Sodium: 655mg
fibre: 3g

Halloumi Fries

Serves: 4

Cook time: 10 mins

Ingredients:

- 35g plain flour
- 235g halloumi cheese
- 1 tsp garlic powder
- Sprinkle of salt and pepper
- Spray oil
- Optional: 1 tsp smoked paprika

Instructions:

1. Slice the halloumi cheese into 1-2 cm sticks.
2. In a mixing bowl, combine the plain flour, garlic powder, salt, and pepper (and smoked

paprika, if using).
3. Preheat the air fryer to 200°C.
4. Dredge the halloumi sticks in the flour mixture, making sure each stick is well coated.
5. Arrange the halloumi in a single layer in the air fryer basket.
6. Spray the halloumi with cooking oil to help it crisp up.
7. Cook the halloumi fries in the air fryer for 6-10 minutes, or until golden brown and crispy.
8. Serve hot, with your choice of dipping sauce.

Per serving:

Calories: 226 Carbohydrates:6g Protein:14g Fat:17g Cholesterol:41 mg Sodium: 858mg fibre: 0.5g

Prosciutto Wrapped Asparagus

Serves: 2

Ingredients:
- 300g asparagus spears, trimmed
- 8 slices of prosciutto

Instructions:
1. Preheat the air fryer to 180°C.
2. Wrap each asparagus spear with a slice of prosciutto.
3. Place the prosciutto-wrapped asparagus in the air fryer basket.
4. Cook for 5 minutes or until the asparagus is tender and the prosciutto is crispy.
5. Serve hot.

Per serving:

Calories: 193 Carbohydrates:7g Protein:17g Fat:11g Cholesterol:41 mg Sodium: 822mg fibre: 2.7g

Crispy Chickpeas

Serves: 2

Cook time: 15 mins

Ingredients:
- 250g chickpeas, drained and dried
- 1 tablespoon olive oil
- 1/2 teaspoon garlic powder
- 1/2 teaspoon smoked paprika
- 1/4 teaspoon black pepper

Instructions:
1. Preheat the air fryer to 90°C.
2. Put the dried chickpeas in the air fryer basket and cook for 12-15 minutes, shaking the basket every 5 minutes to ensure even cooking.
3. In a mixing bowl, combine the olive oil, garlic powder, smoked paprika, and black pepper.
4. Once the chickpeas are cooked, transfer them to the mixing bowl with the spice mixture and toss until the chickpeas are evenly coated.
5. Return the chickpeas to the air fryer basket and cook at 180°C for an additional 2-3 minutes, or until they are crispy and golden brown.
6. Serve immediately as a snack or as a topping for salads or bowls.

Per serving (based on 2 Servings):

Calories: 247 Carbohydrates:29g Protein:11g Fat:10g Sodium: 21mg fibre: 9g

Chapter 8 Desserts

Air Fryer Chocolate Chip Cookies

Serves: 6-8

Cook time: 8-10 mins

Ingredients:
- 100g unsalted butter, softened
- 75g granulated sweetener
- 1 large egg
- 1 tsp vanilla extract
- 140g plain flour
- 1/2 tsp baking soda
- 1/4 tsp salt
- 80g sugar-free chocolate chips

Instructions:
1. Preheat the air fryer to 175°C.
2. In a mixing bowl, cream together the butter and sweetener until light and fluffy.
3. Beat in the egg and vanilla extract until well combined.
4. In another bowl, whisk together the flour, baking soda, and salt.
5. Gradually stir in the dry Ingredients to the wet Ingredients until a dough forms.
6. Fold in the chocolate chips.
7. Divide the dough into 6-8 equal-sized balls and place them in the air fryer basket.
8. Flatten each ball slightly with the palm of your hand.
9. Air fry for 8-10 minutes, or until golden brown and crispy on the outside.
10. Let the cookies cool on a wire rack before serving. Enjoy!

Per serving:
Calories: 122, Carbohydrates:12g Protein:2.3g Fat:7.5g Cholesterol:26mg Sodium: 74mg, fibre: 1g

Diabetic-Friendly Flapjacks

Serves: 4

Cook time: 20 mins

Ingredients:
- 100 g unsalted butter
- 50 g brown sugar substitute (such as Splenda)
- 250 g rolled oats
- 2 tbsp sugar-free maple syrup

Instructions:
1. Chop butter into pieces and put it in the air fryer to melt at 180°C. (1-2 minutes)
2. Mix the rolled oats, brown sugar substitute, and sugar-free maple syrup together in a separate bowl.
3. Add the oat mixture to the melted butter in the pan and mix well.
4. Cook at a reduced temperature of 160°C for 12-15 minutes, or until golden brown.

Per serving(based on 4 Servings)
Calories: 319, Carbohydrates:32g Protein:6g Fat:19g Cholesterol:37mg Sodium: 5mg, fibre: 4g

Diabetic-Friendly Shortbread

Serves: 5

Cook time: 10 mins

Ingredients:
- 85 g unsalted butter
- 30 g powdered erythritol or stevia
- 95 g almond flour
- 1/4 tsp salt

Instructions:
1. In a mixing bowl, beat the unsalted butter

and powdered erythritol or stevia until creamy and well combined.
2. Add the almond flour and salt to the mixing bowl and gently mix until a dough forms. Be careful not to overmix.
3. Form a ball from the dough.
4. Wrap the ball in cling film and place in the fridge for 1-2 hours.
5. When ready, take the dough from the fridge and slice into 1 cm disks.
6. Line the air fryer basket with greaseproof paper.
7. Place the shortbread disks in a lined air fryer basket. Leave plenty of space between each disk.
8. Cook at 170°C for 8-10 minutes or until the edges are lightly golden.
9. After cooling in the air fryer basket for at least 5 minutes, place the biscuits on a wire cooling rack to further cool.

Per serving:

Calories: 200, Carbohydrates:5g Protein:4g Fat:19g Cholesterol:27mg Sodium: 98mg, fibre: 2g

Apple and Mixed Berry Crumble (Diabetic-Friendly)

Serves: 4

Cook time: 15 - 20 mins

Ingredients:

- Fruit Base
- 300 g apples
- 150 g mixed berries (frozen berries will work too)
- 50 g granulated sweetener
- 1 tsp cinnamon
- Crumble
- 200 g almond flour
- 100 g butter (soft)
- 50 g granulated sweetener
- 50 g oats
- Served with sugar-free whipped cream, low-sugar ice cream or custard.

Instructions:

1. Peel apples and dice very finely.
2. Mix berries, apple slices, sweetener, and cinnamon together.
3. Put the berry mix into your dish.
4. In a separate bowl, rub the almond flour and butter together until they have a crumbly texture.
5. Thoroughly mix the sweetener and oats into this mixture.
6. Spoon the crumble over the berry and apple.
7. Place the dish in the air fryer at 180°C for about 15 - 20 minutes. The crumble topping should have a golden glow to it.
8. Serve with a choice of sugar-free whipped cream, low-sugar ice cream or custard.

Per serving:

Calories: 326, Carbohydrates:28g Protein:7g Fat:24g Cholesterol:41mg Sodium: 103mg, fibre: 7g

Diabetic-Friendly Chocolate Cake

Serves: 4

Cook time: 45 - 50 mins

Ingredients:

- 70 g unsweetened applesauce
- 3 large eggs
- 120 g granulated sweetener (e.g. stevia)
- 100 g self-raising flour
- 30 g cocoa powder
- 60 ml sunflower oil
- 40 g chopped walnuts

Instructions:

1. Preheat the air fryer to 200°C.

2. Mix the flour, eggs, sweetener, cocoa powder, applesauce, and oil in a mixing bowl.
3. Use a hand blender on a medium speed to mix the Ingredients together.
4. Fold in walnuts to mix.
5. Line a cake tin with greaseproof paper.
6. Pour the batter into the lined tin.
7. Cover with tin foil and add to air fryer.
8. Reduce temperature to 180°C and cook for 45 minutes.
9. Cook until a knife comes out clean and clear from the centre of the cake.
10. Cool on a wire rack before serving.

Per serving:

Calories: 311, Carbohydrates:24g Protein:6g Fat:23g Cholesterol: 106mg Sodium: 45mg, fibre: 4g

Dried Strawberries

Serves: 3

Cook time: 1 hour

Ingredients:

- 200 g frozen strawberries
- 1-2 tsp sugar substitute (such as stevia) (optional)

Instructions:

1. Preheat the air fryer to the lowest possible setting.
2. Remove stems and slice strawberries very thinly.
3. Sprinkle sliced strawberries with sugar substitute (optional).
4. Arrange strawberry slices in air fryer basket.
5. Cook for one hour at 90°C, turning them at the 30 minute mark.

Per serving:

Calories: 28, Carbohydrates:6g Protein:1g Fat:0g Sodium: 24mg fibre: 2g

Blueberry Lemon Bars

Serves: 8

Cook time: 20 mins

Ingredients:

- For the crust:
- 100 g almond flour
- 50 g coconut flour
- 60 ml coconut oil
- 2 tbsp honey
- For the filling:
- 2 large eggs
- Juice and zest of 1 lemon
- 50 g coconut flour
- 150 g fresh blueberries
- 1 tbsp honey

Instructions:

1. Preheat the air fryer to 180°C.
2. Mix almond flour, coconut flour, coconut oil and honey together until well combined.
3. Line a baking dish with baking paper.
4. Press the crust mixture evenly onto the bottom of the baking dish.
5. Bake crust in air fryer at 180°C for 5 - 8 minutes.
6. In a separate bowl, mix eggs, lemon juice, lemon zest, coconut flour and honey together until well combined.
7. Fold in blueberries.
8. Pour the filling onto the baked crust.
9. Bake in air fryer at 180°C for 15 - 20 minutes.
10. Let cool before slicing into 8 bars.

Per serving:

Calories: 210, Carbohydrates:16g Protein:2g Fat:15g Cholesterol: 47mg Sodium: 24mg, fibre: 4g

Chapter 9 Bonus Recipes

Banana Oat Cookies

Serves: 8

Cook time: 10 - 12 mins

Ingredients:
- 2 ripe bananas
- 160 g oats
- 1 tbsp honey
- 1/2 tsp cinnamon

Instructions:
1. Preheat the air fryer to 160°C.
2. Peel and mash bananas in a mixing bowl.
3. Add the oats, honey and cinnamon to the mashed bananas and mix well.
4. Form small balls from the mixture.
5. Place balls on a lined air fryer basket.
6. Gently press down on each ball with a fork.
7. Bake in the air fryer for 10-12 minutes.
8. Let the cookies cool on the basket for 5 minutes before removing them to a wire rack.
9. Serve once completely cool.

Per serving:
Calories: 92, Carbohydrates:19g Protein:2g Fat:1g Cholesterol: 0mg Sodium: 1mg, fibre: 2g

Crab Cakes

Serves: 4 - 6

Cook time: 8 - 10 mins

Ingredients:
- 455 g crabmeat (fresh or canned)
- 120 g light mayonnaise
- 50 g diced onion
- 40 g diced red pepper
- 2 cloves of garlic, minced
- 2 tbsp Dijon mustard
- 1 tsp paprika
- 30 g whole wheat Panko breadcrumbs
- 1 egg
- Salt and pepper, to taste
- 1 tbsp olive oil

Instructions:
1. In a mixing bowl, combine the crabmeat, light mayonnaise, onion, red pepper, garlic, Dijon mustard, paprika, whole wheat Panko, egg, salt and pepper.
2. Mix well, then form the mixture into cakes, about 8 cm in diameter.
3. Preheat the air fryer to 200°C and lightly brush the basket with olive oil to prevent sticking.
4. Place the crab cakes in the air fryer basket, making sure not to overcrowd it.
5. Cook the crab cakes at 180°C for 8-10 minutes or until golden brown and crispy.

Per serving(1 crab cake, based on 6 Servings):
Calories: 174, Carbohydrates:7g Protein:16g Fat: 9g Cholesterol: 96mg Sodium: 489mg, fibre: 0g

Air Fryer Fish and Chips

Serves: 2

Cook time: 10 mins

Ingredients:
- 2 white fish fillets
- 1 egg, beaten
- 40 g almond flour
- 20 g grated Parmesan cheese
- 1 tsp garlic powder
- 1 tsp paprika
- Salt and pepper, to taste
- 1 large sweet potato, cut into fries
- 1 tbsp olive oil

Instructions:
1. Preheat the air fryer to 200°C.
2. In a shallow dish, combine the almond flour, Parmesan cheese, garlic powder, paprika, salt, and pepper.
3. Dip the fish fillets in the beaten egg, then coat in the almond flour mixture.
4. Place the coated fish fillets in the air fryer basket.
5. Toss the sweet potato fries in olive oil, then place in the air fryer basket alongside the fish.
6. Cook for 10 minutes, flipping the fish and fries halfway through cooking, until the fish is cooked through and the fries are crispy.

Per serving:
Calories: 400, Carbohydrates:40g Protein:28g Fat: 15g Cholesterol: 70mg Sodium: 550mg, fibre: 6g

Air Fryer Ratatouille

Serves: 4

Cook time: 25 mins

Ingredients:
- 1 red onion, chopped
- 1 red pepper, chopped
- 1 yellow pepper, chopped
- 1 green pepper, chopped
- 1 courgette, chopped
- 1 aubergine, chopped
- 2 cloves garlic, minced
- 2 tbsp olive oil
- 1 tbsp dried herbs de Provence
- 1/2 tsp salt
- 1/4 tsp black pepper
- 1 can (400 g) diced tomatoes

Instructions:
1. Preheat the air fryer to 200°C.
2. In a large bowl, mix together the chopped red onion, red, yellow, and green peppers, courgette, aubergine, minced garlic, olive oil, dried herbs de Provence, salt, and black pepper.
3. Pour the mixture into the air fryer basket and cook for 20-25 minutes or until the vegetables are tender and lightly browned.
4. Add the diced tomatoes to the air fryer basket and cook for an additional 5 minutes.
5. Serve hot as a side dish or as a main course with crusty bread or over cooked quinoa.

Per serving(based on 4 Servings):
Calories: 156, Carbohydrates:19g Protein:4g Fat: 9g Cholesterol: 0mg Sodium: 341mg, fibre: 7g

Blueberry Muffins

Serves: 6

Cook time: 12-15 minutes

Ingredients:
- 80 g almond flour
- 30 g coconut flour
- 1 tsp baking powder
- ¼ tsp baking soda
- ¼ tsp salt
- 45 g unsweetened applesauce
- 1 large egg
- 40 g plain Greek yogurt
- 30 g erythritol (or sweetener of choice)
- 1 tsp vanilla extract
- 45 g fresh blueberries

Instructions:
1. Preheat the air fryer to 170°C.
2. In a medium mixing bowl, whisk together the almond flour, coconut flour, baking powder, baking soda, and salt.
3. In another bowl, mix together the applesauce, egg, Greek yogurt, sweetener, and vanilla extract.
4. Add the wet mixture to the dry mixture and mix until just combined.
5. Fold in the blueberries.
6. Divide the batter evenly among six silicone muffin cups.
7. Place the muffin cups in the air fryer basket.
8. Cook the muffins for 12-15 minutes or until a toothpick inserted into the center of a muffin comes out clean.
9. Remove the muffins from the air fryer and let them cool for a few minutes before serving.

Per serving(per muffin):
Calories: 143, Carbohydrates:10g Protein:4g Fat: 10g Sodium: 132mg fibre: 3g

Air Fryer Cinnamon Sugar Donut Holes

Serves: 6

Cooking time: 10 minutes

Ingredients:
- 120g almond flour
- 40g coconut flour
- 1/2 tsp baking powder
- 1/4 tsp baking soda
- 1/4 tsp salt
- 1/4 tsp ground cinnamon
- 3 tbsp unsalted butter, melted
- 3 tbsp granulated sweetener
- 1 large egg
- 1 tsp vanilla extract
- 3 tbsp unsweetened almond milk
- For the cinnamon sugar coating:
- 1/4 cup granulated sweetener
- 1 tsp ground cinnamon
- 2 tbsp unsalted butter, melted

Instructions:
1. Preheat the air fryer to 180°C.
2. In a large bowl, whisk together the almond flour, coconut flour, baking powder, baking soda, salt, and cinnamon.
3. In a separate bowl, whisk together the melted butter, granulated sweetener, egg, vanilla extract, and almond milk.
4. Pour the wet Ingredients into the dry Ingredients and stir until well combined.
5. Scoop tablespoon-sized portions of the dough and roll them into balls.
6. Place the dough balls into the air fryer basket, making sure to leave some space between each one.
7. Cook the donut holes for 8-10 minutes, until they are golden brown and cooked through.
8. While the donut holes are cooking, mix together the granulated sweetener and

cinnamon in a small bowl.
9. When the donut holes are done, remove them from the air fryer and brush them with the melted butter.
10. Roll the donut holes in the cinnamon sugar mixture until they are coated.
11. Serve the donut holes warm.

Per serving:
Calories: 196, Carbohydrates: 7g Protein:6g Fat: 17g Cholesterol: 52mg Sodium: 243mg, fibre: 3g

Granola

Serves: 6

Cooking time: 10-15 minutes

Ingredients:
- 1.3 kg rolled oats
- 230 g chopped nuts (almonds, walnuts, pecans, etc.)
- 115 g shredded coconut
- 60 g natural sweetener (stevia or erythritol)
- 30 g oil (coconut, avocado, or vegetable oil)
- 5 ml vanilla extract
- ½ tsp salt

Instructions:
1. In a large bowl, mix together the oats, nuts, and coconut.
2. In a separate bowl, mix together the natural sweetener, oil, vanilla extract, and salt.
3. Pour the wet Ingredients over the dry Ingredients and stir until everything is evenly coated.
4. Spread the mixture evenly in the basket of the air fryer.
5. Cook at 150°C for 10-15 minutes, stirring every 5 minutes, or until the granola is golden brown and crispy.
6. Carefully remove the granola from the air fryer and let it cool completely before storing it in an airtight container.

Per serving: (based on 6 Servings):
Calories: 510, Carbohydrates: 54g Protein:14g Fat: 28g Cholesterol: 0mg Sodium: 193mg, fibre: 10g

Breakfast Energy Balls

Serves: 5

Cooking time: 5-7 minutes

Ingredients:
- 80 g rolled oats
- 70 g natural almond butter (without added sugar)
- 130 g natural sweetener (stevia or erythritol)
- 1 tsp vanilla extract
- 35 g sugar-free chocolate chips
- 25 g unsweetened shredded coconut

Instructions:
1. In a medium bowl, mix together the oats, almond butter, natural sweetener, vanilla extract, chocolate chips, and shredded coconut.
2. Roll the mixture into balls and place them in the air fryer basket.
3. Preheat your air fryer to 180C and cook the balls for 5-7 minutes, or until heated through.

Per serving: (based on 5 Servings):
Calories: 252, Carbohydrates: 30g Protein: 7g Fat: 12g Cholesterol: 0mg Sodium: 26mg , fibre: 4g

Air Fryer Diabetic-Friendly Soda Bread

Serves: 8

Cooking time: 20 minutes

Ingredients:
- 240g wholemeal flour
- 60g plain flour
- 1 tsp baking soda
- 1/2 tsp salt
- 1 tbsp unsalted butter, softened
- 1 tbsp honey
- 240ml unsweetened almond milk
- 1 egg
- 1 tbsp apple cider vinegar

Instructions:
1. In a mixing bowl, whisk together the wholemeal flour, plain flour, baking soda, and salt.
2. In a separate bowl, cream together the softened butter and honey until light and fluffy.
3. Add the almond milk, egg, and apple cider vinegar to the butter mixture and whisk until well combined.
4. Pour the wet Ingredients into the dry Ingredients and mix until just combined.
5. Knead the dough lightly until it comes together, then shape it into a round loaf and place it in the air fryer basket.
6. Cook at 190°C for 20 minutes, or until the bread is golden brown and sounds hollow when tapped.
7. Let the bread cool on a wire rack before slicing and serving.

Per serving:
Calories: 140, Carbohydrates: 5g Protein: 5g Fat: 3.5g   Sodium: 250mg fibre: 4g

Air Fryer Diabetic-Friendly Soda Bread

Serves: 4

Cooking time: 12 minutes

Ingredients:
- 4 boneless, skinless chicken breasts (120g each)
- 2 tbsp pesto
- 1 tbsp olive oil
- 1/2 tsp garlic powder
- 1/4 tsp salt
- 1/4 tsp black pepper
- 2 tbsp grated Parmesan cheese
- 25 g almond flour

Instructions:
1. Cut the chicken breasts into bite-sized pieces and place them in a mixing bowl.
2. Add the pesto, olive oil, garlic powder, salt, and black pepper to the bowl and toss to coat the chicken.
3. In a separate bowl, mix together the grated Parmesan cheese and almond flour.
4. Dip each chicken piece into the Parmesan-almond flour mixture, making sure it's coated on all sides.
5. Preheat the air fryer to 375°F (190°C) for 5 minutes.
6. Place the coated chicken pieces in the air fryer basket in a single layer, making sure they don't touch each other.
7. Cook for 12 minutes, shaking the basket halfway through, until the chicken is cooked through and golden brown.
8. Serve hot with additional pesto for dipping, if desired.

Per serving:
Calories: 240, Carbohydrates: 3g Protein: 35g Fat: 10g Sodium: 330mg fibre: 2g

Air Fryer Cinnamon Sweet Potato Wedges

Serves: 4

Cooking time: 20 minutes

Ingredients:
- 2 medium sweet potatoes (500g), peeled and cut into wedges
- 1 tbsp olive oil
- 1 tsp ground cinnamon
- 1/4 tsp salt
- 1/4 tsp black pepper

Instructions:
1. Preheat the air fryer to 190°C for 5 minutes.
2. In a mixing bowl, toss the sweet potato wedges with olive oil, cinnamon, salt, and black pepper until well coated.
3. Arrange the sweet potato wedges in a single layer in the air fryer basket. You may need to cook them in batches.
4. Cook for 10 minutes, then flip the wedges and cook for another 10 minutes until crispy and tender.
5. Serve hot as a side dish or snack.

Per serving:
Calories: 120, Carbohydrates: 2g Protein: 2g Fat: 3.5g Sodium: 180mg fibre: 4g

Cinnamon Roasted Almonds

Prep time: 5 mins Cook time: 8 mins Serves: 4

Ingredients:
- ½ teaspoon cinnamon
- 1 tablespoon sugar
- 30 g butter
- 130 g whole almonds

Instructions:
1. Melt butter in microwave or over a low heat.
2. Add almonds, sugar and cinnamon to the butter and mix well ensuring all nuts are well coated.
3. Arrange almonds in air fryer basket so none are overlapping.
4. Place in an air fryer at 200°C for 4 minutes.
5. After 4 minutes stir almonds and put them back in air fryer for another 4 minutes.
6. Allow to cool before eating.

Per serving:
Calories: 254, Carbohydrates: 10g Protein: 7g Fat: 22g Sodium: 44mg fibre: 4.2g

30-Day Meal Plan

DAY 1	DAY 2	DAY 3	DAY 4
1.Air Fryer Breakfast Burrito	1.Air Fryer Cinnamon French Toast Sticks	1.Air Fryer Omelette	1.Air Fryer Breakfast Hash
2.Crispy Prawn Cakes	2.Chicken Breasts	2.Air Fryer Crispy Tofu	2.Air Fryer Fish Fillets
3.Roasted Cauliflower Steaks	3.Air Fryer Beef and Vegetable Kabobs	3.Garlic Butter Prawn Skewers	3.Vegetable Fajitas
4.Airfryer Quinoa and Black Bean Cakes	4.Fish Fingers	4.Air Fryer Green Beans	4.Cauliflower Buffalo Wings
DAY 5	**DAY 6**	**DAY 7**	**DAY 8**
1.Air Fryer Cinnamon French Toast	1Air Fryer Egg and Veggie Muffins	1.Air Fryer Sweet Potato Toast	1.Air Fryer Blueberry Muffins
2.Grilled Lemon Herb Halibut	2.Turkey and Vegetable Skillet	2.Roasted Brussels Sprouts and Sweet Potatoes	2.Air Fryer Salmon
3.Air Fryer Beef Fajitas	3.Air Fryer Salmon with Lemon and Dill	3.Cajun Tilapia /Stuffed Portobello Mushrooms	3.Air Fryer Lamb Chops with Garlic and Rosemary
4.Air Fryer Mozzarella Sticks	4.Air Fryer Pita Chips	4.Crispy Brussels Sprouts Chips	4.Air Fryer Vegetable Spring Rolls
DAY 9	**DAY 10**	**DAY 11**	**DAY 12**
1.Air Fryer French Toast Sticks	1.Air Fryer Breakfast Sausage Patties	1.Air Fryer Cinnamon Apple Chips	1.Air Fryer Breakfast Stuffed Peppers
2.Air Fryer Turkey Burgers	2.Roasted Brussel Sprouts	2.Air Fryer Pork Chops	2.Garlic Roasted Carrots
3.Garlic Parmesan Crusted Salmon	3.Greek-Style Lamb Kabobs with Tzatziki	3.Baked Sweet Potato Falafel	3.Air Fryer Pork Chops
4.Sweet Potato Tater Tots	4.Air Fryer Onion Rings	4.Air Fryer Sausage Rolls	4.Air Fryer 'Roasted' Peppers
DAY 13	**DAY 14**	**DAY 15**	**DAY 16**
1.Air Fryer Banana Oatmeal Muffins	1Air Fryer Turkey and Spinach Frittata	1.Air Fryer Blueberry Scones	1.Air Fryer Sweet Potato Hash Browns
2.Air Fryer Beef Kabobs	2.Air Fryer Asparagus	2.Air Fryer Pork Tenderloin	2Lemon Garlic Baked Cod
3.Courgette Fritters	3.Air Fryer Lamb Kofta	3.Salmon with Lemon-Dill Sauce	3.Air Fryer Chicken Thighs
4.Tuna Melt	4.Calzone	4.Halloumi Fries	4.Prosciutto Wrapped Asparagus

DAY 17	DAY 18	DAY 19	DAY 20
1.Air Fryer Greek Omelette	1.Air Fryer Coconut Flour Pancakes	1.Air Fryer Apple Cinnamon Oatmeal	1.Air Fryer Baked Oats
2.Air Fryer Chicken Parmesan	2.Air Fryer Tuna Steaks with Sesame Seeds	2.Crispy salmon with lemon and dill	2.Air Fryer Beef and Broccoli Stir-Fry
3.Air Fryer Coconut Prawns	3.Air Fryer Pork Chops with Mustard Crust	3.Stuffed Courgettes	3.Air Fryer Veggie Skewers
4.Crispy Chickpeas	4.Air Fryer Chocolate Chip Cookies	4.Cinnamon Roasted Almonds	4.Air Fryer Diabetic-Friendly Soda Bread

DAY 21	DAY 22	DAY 23	DAY 24
1.Air Fryer Breakfast Quiche	1.Air Fryer Breakfast Burritos	1.Air Fryer Breakfast Burrito	1.Air Fryer Cinnamon French Toast Sticks
2.Air Fryer Lemon Garlic Chicken	2.Roasted Vegetables	2.Air Fryer Fish Tacos with Mango Salsa	2.Air Fryer Lemon Herb Salmon with Roasted Vegetables
3.Air Fryer Blackened Salmon	3.Air Fryer Turkey Breast	3.Honey Garlic Pork Chops	3.Air Fryer Lemon and Herb Chicken Thighs
4.Air Fryer Cinnamon Sweet Potato Wedges	4.Air Fryer Diabetic-Friendly Soda Bread	4.Breakfast Energy Balls	4.Granola

DAY 25	DAY 26	DAY 27	DAY 28
1.Air Fryer Omelette	1.Air Fryer Breakfast Hash	1.Air Fryer Cinnamon French Toast	1.Air Fryer Banana Oatmeal Muffins
2.Air Fryer Veggie Burger	2.Garlic Prawns and Broccoli	2.Air Fryer Chicken Fajitas	2.Airfryer Pork Tenderloin with Herbs and Garlic
3. Air Fryer Tandoori Chicken Skewers	3.Air Fryer Pork Belly Bites	3.Air Fryer Tofu and Broccoli	3.Air Fryer Tuna Steaks with Lemon and Herbs
4.Air Fryer Cinnamon Sugar Donut Holes	4.Blueberry Muffins	4.Air Fryer Fish and Chips	4.Air Fryer Ratatouille

DAY 29	DAY 30		
1.Air Fryer Breakfast Sausage Patties	1.Air Fryer Cinnamon Apple Chips		
2.Air Fryer Mackerel Fillets	2.Garlic and Herb Prawn Skewers		
3.Air Fryer Pork Meatballs	3.Air Fryer BBQ Chicken Wings		
4.Crab Cakes	4.Banana Oat Cookies		

Index

A

Air Fryer Apple Cinnamon Oatmeal 15
Air Fryer Asian Beef Skewers 47
Air Fryer Asparagus 53
Air Fryer Baked Oats 15
Airfryer Baked Potatoes 55
Air Fryer Banana Oatmeal Muffins 12
Air Fryer Battered Fish 30
Air Fryer BBQ Chicken Wings 35
Air Fryer Beef and Broccoli Stir-Fry 20
Air Fryer Beef and Vegetable Kabobs 45
Air Fryer Beef Fajitas 45
Air Fryer Beef Jerky 46
Air Fryer Beef Kabobs 19
Air Fryer Beef Kofta 47
Air Fryer Blackened Salmon 29
Air Fryer Blueberry Muffins 10
Air Fryer Blueberry Scones 13
Air Fryer Breakfast Burrito 7
Air Fryer Breakfast Burritos 16
Air Fryer Breakfast Hash 8
Air Fryer Breakfast Quiche 16
Air Fryer Breakfast Sausage Patties 10
Air Fryer Breakfast Stuffed Peppers 11
Airfryer Cajun Chicken Thighs 38
Air Fryer Chicken Fajitas 23
Air Fryer Chicken Parmesan 19
Air Fryer Chicken Satay 35
Air Fryer Chicken Satay Skewers 36

Air Fryer Chicken Sliders 61
Air Fryer Chicken Thighs 19
Air Fryer Chocolate Chip Cookies 65
Air Fryer Cinnamon Apple Chips 11
Air Fryer Cinnamon French Toast 8
Air Fryer Cinnamon French Toast Sticks 7
Air Fryer Cinnamon Sugar Donut Holes 70
Air Fryer Cinnamon Sweet Potato Wedges 73
Airfryer Classic Potato Fries 55
Air Fryer Coconut Flour Pancakes 14
Air Fryer Coconut Prawns 30
Airfryer Crispy Kale 56
Air Fryer Crispy Tofu 48
Air Fryer Diabetic-Friendly Soda Bread 72
Air Fryer Duck Breast with Orange Glaze 33
Air Fryer Egg and Veggie Muffins 9
Air Fryer Fish and Chips 69
Air Fryer Fish Fillets 17
Air Fryer Fish Tacos with Mango Salsa 21
Air Fryer Fish Tempura 31
Air Fryer French Toast Sticks 10
Airfryer Garlic Mushrooms 54
Air Fryer Garlic Rosemary Turkey Breast 40
Air Fryer Greek Lamb Chops 44
Air Fryer Greek Omelette 14
Air Fryer Green Beans 53
Airfryer Herb Roasted Potatoes 55
Air Fryer Lamb Chops with Garlic and Rosemary 43
Air Fryer Lamb Kofta 44
Air Fryer Lemon and Herb Chicken Thighs 34
Air Fryer Lemon Garlic Chicken 21
Air Fryer Lemon Garlic Salmon 31

• 76 •

Air Fryer Lemon Garlic Turkey Breast 34
Air Fryer Lemon Herb Salmon with Roasted Vegetables 22
Air Fryer Lemon Pepper Chicken 37
Air Fryer Mackerel Fillets 28
Air Fryer Moroccan Lamb Meatballs 45
Air Fryer Mozzarella Sticks 58
Air Fryer Omelette 8
Air Fryer Onion Rings: 61
Air Fryer Pita Chips 59
Air Fryer Pork Belly Bites 41
Air Fryer Pork Chops 18, 41
Air Fryer Pork Chops with Mustard Crust 42
Air Fryer Pork Meatballs 42
Air Fryer Pork Tenderloin 41
Airfryer Pork Tenderloin with Herbs and Garlic 24
Airfryer Quinoa and Black Bean Cakes 56
Air Fryer Ratatouille 69
Air Fryer 'Roasted' Peppers 62
Air Fryer Salmon 18
Air Fryer Salmon with Lemon and Dill 26
Air Fryer Sausage Rolls 62
Air Fryer Steak 46
Air Fryer Sweet Potato Fries 49
Air Fryer Sweet Potato Hash Browns 13
Air Fryer Sweet Potato Toast 9
Air Fryer Tandoori Chicken Skewers: 22
Air Fryer Teriyaki Chicken Thighs 40
Airfryer Teriyaki Turkey Meatballs 39
Air Fryer Tofu and Broccoli 52
Air Fryer Trout with Lemon and Thyme 28
Air Fryer Tuna Fish Cakes 32

Air Fryer Tuna Steaks with Lemon and Herbs 29
Air Fryer Tuna Steaks with Sesame Seeds 29
Air Fryer Turkey and Spinach Frittata 12
Air Fryer Turkey Breast 33
Air Fryer Turkey Burgers 18, 36
Air Fryer Turkey Meatballs 37
Air Fryer Turkey Meatballs with Zucchini Noodles 24
Airfryer Vegetable Pakoras 56
Air Fryer Vegetable Spring Rolls: 60
Air Fryer Veggie Burger 51
Air Fryer Veggie Skewers 54
Apple and Mixed Berry Crumble (Diabetic-Friendly) 66

B

Baked Sweet Potato Falafel 49
Banana Oat Cookies 68
Blueberry Lemon Bars 67
Blueberry Muffins 70
Breakfast Energy Balls 71

C

Cajun Tilapia 26
Calzone 63
Cauliflower Buffalo Wings 58
Chicken Breasts 17
Chicken Kiev 39
Chicken Tenders 33
Cinnamon Roasted Almonds 73
Courgette Fritters 50
Crab Cakes 68

Crispy Brussels Sprouts Chips   59

Crispy Chickpeas   64

Crispy Duck Legs: 38

Crispy Prawn Cakes   25

Crispy salmon with lemon and dill   28

D

Diabetic-Friendly Chocolate Cake   66

Diabetic-Friendly Flapjacks   65

Diabetic-Friendly Shortbread 65

Dried Strawberries   67

F

Fish Fingers   57

G

Garlic and Herb Prawn Skewers   25

Garlic Butter Prawn Skewers: 25

Garlic Parmesan Crusted Salmon   26

Garlic Prawns and Broccoli   23

Garlic Roasted Carrots   53

Granola   71

Greek-Style Lamb Kabobs with Tzatziki   43

Grilled Lemon Herb Halibut   27

H

Halloumi Fries   63

Honey Garlic Pork Chops   42

Honey Mustard Turkey Breast: 38

L

Lemon Garlic Baked Cod   27

M

Moroccan-Spiced Air Fryer Lamb Chops   44

O

Oat-Coated Fish   30

P

Porridge Bread   57

Prosciutto Wrapped Asparagus   64

R

Roasted Brussel Sprouts   52

Roasted Brussels Sprouts and Sweet Potatoes   50

Roasted Cauliflower Steaks   48

Roasted Vegetables   50

S

Salmon with Lemon-Dill Sauce   20

Spicy Prawns: 32

Stuffed Courgettes   54

Stuffed Portobello Mushrooms   51

Sweet Potato Tater Tots   60

T

Tuna Melt   62

Turkey and Vegetable Skillet   17

V

Vegetable Fajitas   48

Printed in Great Britain
by Amazon